KARL LENK

THE MAURITIUS AFFAIR
The Boat People of 1940/41

KÜRT
MAURITIUS
OKT. 1982

43/250

R.S.Lenk

Edited and translated from the original German
by R.S. Lenk

British Library Cataloguing and Publication Data
A Catalogue record of this book is available from the British Library.

Published by R.S. Lenk
2A Crescent Close
Woodingdean
Brighton BN2 6SR
Publisher's Prefix 0-9518805

Printed and bound in Great Britain by Booksprint
30 Clerkenwell Close, London EC1R 0AT
MCMXCIII

DEDICATION

This book is dedicated to the memory of my father, to his erstwhile shipmates and fellow detainees, their descendants, and to all those who have suffered at the hands of tyrannical régimes and who embarked upon hazardous journeys to escape persecution.

R.S. Lenk,
July 1993

Karl Lenk in 1936

Acknowledgements

I gratefully acknowledge the work which my friend Bob Symonds has so very kindly undertaken to produce a camera-ready typesetting, to Mme. Geneviève Pitot: for all her ceaseless archival research, to the publishers of the *Jewish Chronicle* and to all those others whose permission to reproduce previously published material I have sought and which covers the following items:

"King Opposed Aliyah" (Jewish Chronicle Reporter, *Jewish Chronicle* dated March 6th, 1981); "Obedient servants" (Julia Pascal, *Jewish Chronicle* dated January 8th, 1993 and two photographs forming part of the same article, the copyright of Messrs. Rex Features of London); the editorial entitled "One plus one plus one" (*Jewish Chronicle* dated January 8th, 1993) and "History lessons (Vernon Bogdanor, *Jewish Chronicle* dated January 29th, 1993).

I also wish to thank those (notably Mme. G. Pitot) who have supplied me with photographs of Mauritius, some of them of the prison at Beau Bassin, which were taken by an anonymous photographer, to Mr. Perez B. Mayer of Israel for his wonderful woodcuts of scenes from the "Atlantic" and of the prison camp at Beau Bassin, to Mr. Kürt for his portrait drawing of my father dated October 1942, to Mr. F. Haendel who produced the splendidly satirical pen-and-wash drawings of a Greek trader taking watches and fountain pens in payment for some grapes, as well as the two magnificent woodcuts of a British officer and a couple of other-ranks in Palestine (1943). Last, but not least, I wish to thank all the publishers who have consistently turned down the manuscript for many decades with generous good wishes for its success. This has enabled me to accumulate much additional material, including some that has come from my own pen and which, in retrospect, is entirely relevant to the events of which this story is a significant part.

R.S. Lenk, July 1993

Contents

Synopsis 7

Foreword 9

1. Preparations 11

2. Bratislava 19

3. "Helios" 37

4. "Atlantic" 42

5. Cyprus and Haifa Harbour 61

6. Akko and Atlit 67

7. "Nieuw Zeeland" 75

8. Beau Bassin 80

9. Postscript 85

COMMENTS FROM THE PRESS

'King opposed aliyah' 91

Bevin and the Jews 92

Obedient Servants 95

Guernsey's Shame 98

One plus one plus one 100

History Lesson 102

THREE ENGLISH POEMS

1. The Survivor 105

2. The Silent Stage 106

3. The Epitaph 106

POEMS IN GERMAN

GERMANY

Sinaifahrt 107

Deutschland 108

Elbequelle 109

Bergen Belsen 110

Ohlsdorf 112

Nach Berlin! 113

Osterspaziergang 116

AUSTRIA

Wiedersehen 117

Mauthausener Epitaph 118

Der Nachkriegsrückkehrer—50 Jahre
  später 119

Das Problem des anständigen
  Durchschnittbürgers 120

Der kleine Nazi—er ist es noch immer! ... 121

REFLECTIONS

Gefährliche Ruhe 122

Wo? Wann? Warum? 123

Ausflug 124

Trügerischer Frähling 125

LITERATURE 126

A List of Some of the Names Mentioned
  in this Document 127

Synopsis

This book is based upon Karl Lenk's diaries. It describes his attempts to escape from Nazi-occupied Austria before and after the outbreak of war and to join his family who had succeeded in reaching Yugoslavia and who eventually found refuge in England.

After war had been declared the writer made a number of abortive attempts to cross the Yugoslav border illegally. The situation in Vienna and the pressure on the Jews are described. In the end Karl Lenk joined an illegal transport to Palestine where his brother, a distinguished radiologist, had emigrated. The transport left Vienna in the late autumn of 1939 but was held up in Bratislava for many months. Eventually the transport continued down river on a Danube steamer, people were transferred to a derelict Greek tramp ship, passed through the Bosphorus and the Dardanelles and hugged the Greek islands of the Aegean. Overcrowded, short of fuel and provisions, water and medical supplies, and buffeted by storms, the refugees seized control from the treacherous and pusillanimous Greek captain and cannibalised the ship's timbers for fuel. Meanwhile the German invasion of Greece and Crete was in full swing and naval battles were being fought out in the Mediterranean.

Having miraculously reached Cyprus the refugees were not allowed ashore. They were forced to proceed to Haifa under a British naval escort where they witnessed the blowing up of the "Patria" in the harbour. They were taken to prison camps in Akko and Atlit where they were roughly handled by Palestine police. They were shipped to the island of Mauritius where they were imprisoned for the duration and where many died from typhoid, malaria or dysentery. Karl Lenk succumbed to a bacterial infection after one year in the island prison, just as he had gradually recovered from emaciation and from the effects of the severe bronchitis from which he had been suffering throughout most of the journey.

Camp life is described, warts and all, but at no stage is the account tendentious or rancorous; it is factual and events are allowed to speak for themselves. In addition, there are a number of original documents, newspaper excerpts, photographs, drawings, woodcuts and a list of references. These afford a rare insight into the thinking of the British establishment of the day. Also included are letters of condolence and a list of names which may be of interest to ex-fellow refugees, their friends and descendants.

I have added some relevant poetry of my own. Some of the poems are written in English and some in German. Inasmuch as my formative years fell within the cataclysmic period of World War II, I beg the readers' indulgence for taking this liberty as the author's son.

R.S. Lenk

C o p y

Grundnummer 00438778 5 III 36 I.A. 786   No. E: 1169/1912
Abschrift

Geburts — Zeugnis

Von dem Unterzeichneten wird hiemit bezeuget, dass am sechsundzwanzig-

sten des Monates April im Jahre Eintausend Acht ~~Neun~~ — Hundert achtziger

(26.April 1884) dem Herrn, Lenk Edmund .....von seiner Ehegattin....

Eugenie....geborenen...Kohn...in Prag...No.C: 046 — II..ein....Sohn...

geboren und demselben der Name... Karl... beigelegt wurde.

Eingetragen in dem Geburtsprotokolle der israelitischen Kultus —

gemeinde in Prag. Litera XIV Pag. 245 No. 63.

Zur Bestaetigung dessen nachstehende Fertigung nebst Amtssiegel.
Prag, am 12.Juni 1912. Die Matrikenfuehrung der israel.Kultusgemeinde
in Prag. gez. Winternitz unleserl.

Stempel: Matrikenfuehrung d. ~~Matrik~~ israelitischen Kultusgemeinde Prag.

Oesterreichische Stempelmarke 50 Kronen.
Verglichen und stimmt diese Abschrift mit dem mir vorliegendem mit
einer Krone gestempelten Originale vollkommen ueberein. Wien, am
8.November Eintausendneunhundertzweiundzwanzig. Geb. s,Stpl. 1550 K.
                                          Signature Dr.Franz Hansa
Rubber stamp: Mit Dekret des Landesgerichtes Wien vom 21.6.
Carl Neubauer   1922 Pr.3888 bestellter Substitut des oeff.
k.k. Notar in Wien   Notars Carl Neubauer in Wien
Oesterreich u.d.Enns

B-H Bezirkshauptmannschaft Mariahilf-Neubau Annahme des Zusatznamens
Israel — ~~Sara~~ angezeigt!—Wien, am 24.Juni 1939. Der Bezirkshauptmann:
I.A. illegible Rubber stamp: Bezirkshauptmannschaft Mariahilf-
Neubau — Wien

C o p y   c e r t i f i e d   c o r r e c t .

Beau Bassin (Mauritius)
March 9 th 1943.   Area Commandant
                                          Detainment Camp

Plate I: Copy of Birth Certificate of Karl Lenk

FOREWORD

This is a true story. My father's original German narrative comprises 240 pages of manuscript in his own close and beautiful handwriting and is now in the safe keeping of Mme. Françoise Pitot, a Mauritian lady who has devoted her life to the documentation of the Mauritius episode and whose generous friendship I am privileged to share with the other ex-detainees and their families. Although it is a thrilling adventure story, it has never been intended to thrill. It is a document of the time, a record both of brutality and compassion. of greed and generosity, of cowardice and courage, of selfishness and altruism, of meanness and of sacrifice, of desperation and of hope. It is a harrowing tale of unadorned and unsophisticated simplicity.

I am much troubled these days by the spread of indifference to human suffering. There are boat people today, and "prisoners of conscience". Indifference is not a sign of callousness, more a sign of self-induced ignorance, of not wanting to know uncomfortable facts. This has led to a widespread dulling of the sense of morality and an apparent (if unexpressed) acquiescence in what is done in our name to people like ourselves, when an outraged sense of justice should channel righteous indignation into determined protest.

The translation itself presented no problems. There obviously had to be some editing in order to avoid misunderstanding and repetition. I have included some splendid drawings and lino cuts by artists whose identity I have not always been able to establish and to whom I must therefore give anonymous credit with sincere apologies. The name of Fritz Haendel has appeared in one of my father's letters and several linocuts are autographed by Perez B. Mayer.

The story itself is based on a carefully kept diary of events which was lost after the full account had been written. There are repeated references to rumours of swindles and betrayals; whether these have any substance we shall probably never know, but it is understandable that people in distress become suspicious even of their proven friends whenever an already desperate situation is aggravated by yet another calamity. In any case, I did not feel it right to suppress the reported "murmurings of the multitude" since the latter are clearly part of the ambient atmosphere as the drama unfolded and was played out.

As for my father's lost opportunities, I do know of three. On receiving his Permit for entry into the United Kingdom his friends begged him to go at once *to* the British Consulate in Vienna and get his visa rather than wait from Friday till the following Wednesday as instructed. But he had been brought up to obey official instructions and it did not occur to him that five days' delay might be fatal at a time when everybody must have known that war was imminent. We even spoke to him over the telephone from London on the afternoon of August 31st, 1939 which in itself was nothing short of a miracle and implored him to take his passport and his Permit, make for the Belgian border, get his visa in Brussels and arrive safely in England within days. His third and last opportunity came in Atlit. His brother who lived in Haifa at the time sent him a message to report without delay to a certain doctor in the camp who would have certified that he needed hospitalisation, as indeed he did. He never reported for the examination; those who did escaped the subsequent deportation and imprisonment on the island of Mauritius.

We shall never know why he missed out on those opportunities, if indeed such they were. What can be said, however, is that the threat of violence and the effect of psychological pressure were such that no man can say how he would have reacted in similar circumstances.

I have tried to translate and edit the story in a way in which I feel that my father would have wished, had he had the benefit of several decades' historical perspective.

When any people mentioned by name or their descendents and friends read this I hope that they will share my conviction that I have done the right thing in retelling a story which has unfortunately become topical again.

R.S. Lenk, 1993

Karl Lenk with Henny
Schück and friend

Vienna 1939

1. Preparations

Towards the end of September 1938—I believe it was the 25th—my two sons left for Yugoslavia. My wife followed them a few days later. The day before the boys left the younger one played some piece by Chopin which affected me deeply. It was like a song of farewell, full of sadness, longing and renunciation and reflected the mood as I stood on the railway platform on each occasion saying farewell to those I loved. Whenever I think of it the tune echoes within me.

Life thereafter was a succession of fantastic escape schemes which, after laborious preparation, invariably resulted in failure. More about that presently, but let me first tell about two earlier attempts, because they illustrate the desperate need of leaving the country that had been my homeland and that of my fathers for generations.

On March 1st 1939 my brother, having found refuge in Haifa applied through a refugee committee in London to obtain permission for me to come to England and deposited £200 in my name at a London bank, together with an official declaration from the appropriate authorities in Palestine who stated that all the necessary steps were being taken to secure subsequent immigration there. Nearly six months had passed and many people I knew, even some who had applied long after me, had left for England. It normally took about three months to obtain the Permit assuming that the required documents were all in order. But it would appear that two officials were simultaneously handling my application; one of them invariably had the document which the other needed and they were for ever bogged down in internal correspondence. To top it all, one of the senior civil servants at the Home Office whose final endorsement of approval was essential, had apparently gone on a long holiday. The consequences were disastrous. My Permit eventually arrived in Vienna on August 26th 1939, five days before war broke out. The British Consulate was packing and I was unable to obtain my visa. I stood in front of the gates of the Consulate in the Wallnerstrasse which bore the large notice: GESPERRT. How I had been looking forward to the reunion with my family who, after six months in Yugoslavia, had managed to obtain British visas and were now London. A dream, so nearly fulfilled, had melted away, underlining the mocking futility of months of desperate effort. For a few moments—they seemed endless—I leaned against the wall, unable to move and scarcely able to stand. When my physical strength returned my mind remained numb and I did not know where to turn. I walked the streets for hours; suddenly they seemed strange and hostile, as if they were part of a conspiracy with a mocking crowd of local Nazis.

On August 28th Hitler spoke. He promised that, in the event of war, not a single Jew on the continent would survive. War started on September 1st and life in Hitler's Austria, precarious for a Jew up to then, became wellnigh impossible. I was depressed for days and began to resign myself to the prospect of not getting out at all. But then the courage of despair asserted itself and on September 12th I attempted to cross into Yugoslavia in a bid to escape certain death. I spent ten days at the border and at times actually across it, trying to make for Zagreb without an official entry visa. There was a provincial department of the Palestine Office in Vienna which organised such illegal transports and I had been told about it by a lady whom I had met at the home of my elder son's mother-in-law. The lady and her husband were subtenants in her house in the Nusswaldgasse. I remember their garden and talking to my future daughter-in-law about our British visas which were so confidently expected. (She eventually made it to London just a month before war broke out).

The attempt to escape to Yugoslavia was a failure. It transpired later on that the Palestine Office had nothing whatever to do with that transport and that two gentlemen, K. and B. who had been employed there had merely used their positions as a cover for a bit of freelancing to make the set-up look respectable. They had scraped up a number of desperate people who were willing to cough up a minimum of 500 marks each. I had borrowed the money, having already spent every penny in anticipation of my journey to England, so that I had practically nothing left for food, let alone for any fancy escape schemes. To make the transport profitable they intended to send people across the border in batches of 20. To persuade people to go across in such large groups the organisers had promised to refund the money in the event of failure. They tried to justify the high cost by stating that certain Yugoslav border officials had to be "informed" and that there was only about an hour's walk ahead of us. At a certain place— exactly where we were to be told at the border—a coach would be waiting which would pick up 20 people at a time. This proved to be a pack of lies concocted for the sole purpose of attracting customers. I was among the first group; a waiting list for other groups was in the process of being compiled, but after the debacle which followed no further mugs came forward.

The details, briefly, were as follows: On September 12th we were packed into eight taxi cabs and arrived at the border village of Minnihof-Libau nine hours later. The customs house stood in the middle of the road; there was no railway line. It was two in the morning. We trudged through fields and muddy footpaths up steep slopes for about an hour and a half and found a barn at length in which we spent the rest of the night. We returned to the customs house as daylight dawned. Our belongings were taken away. They took my briefcase, which contained a few toiletries and a little underwear on the grounds that one man had more than the permitted amount of luggage. The inspection of the luggage was followed by a strict scrutiny of the passports and a three-hour slog, whereupon we were billeted with three peasants in batches of 20. We now made several attempts at crossing the border. On the first occasion the Yugoslav guards opened fire and one man was hit in the leg. During the following ten days we took shelter in barns, without soap, toothbrushes or shaving kit while making a number of further attempts. The fellow who was supposed to be our guide did no more than casually describing the terrain to us. At length the sergeant of the gendarmerie received orders to arrest us unless we disappeared for good during the following night. Fortunately the guide managed to persuade the authorities to permit us to return to Vienna with our German passports while those of us who were stateless were allowed to keep on trying for another fortnight. In the end our bad luck turned out to be our salvation, for Hitler presently caught up with those who had made it into Yugoslavia.

Though bitterly disappointed at this fresh failure, there was some relief in returning to my flat in Vienna, since arrest at the border would have landed me in a concentration camp. We were told that our money would be refunded in Vienna, minus expenses for food. The leader promised to obtain Yugoslav transit visas for us, after all, but nobody was quite so naive as to believe this. Yet there still seemed to be some faint hope. We agreed to surrender our passport to the leader in return for a receipt endorsed by the burgomaster of the village which stated that the passports had been taken for the purpose of obtaining a Yugoslav visa. That night we took a coach to the nearest railway station and returned to Vienna. The passports were to be collected at the Palestine Office during the following week.

Mr. Rothenberg, the head of the Palestine Office, had got wind of the activities of Messrs. K. and B. Meanwhile K. and B. had moved their "office" to the Franz-Josefs-Kai and we learned a fortnight later that our "leader", an "Aryan" from Graz, had been arrested by the Yugoslav police. The authorities in Zagreb had taken possession of our passports and had handed them to the German consul. The consulate's solicitor was unable to secure the man's release and therefore asked a Jewish lawyer who was in good standing with the local authorities to intercede for the fellow who was eventually allowed to go, in return for which the passports were returned to the Jewish community in Vienna rather than to the Gestapo. Four weeks passed before we got them back. All through that time we expected peremptory invitations from the Gestapo. The Germans did not actually discourage illegal frontier crossings, provided that the exit visa was in order, but the loss of the passport would have been most serious. K. and B. were arrested for their failure to refund the money. One of our group was entrusted with trying to retrieve what he could on behalf of us all. In the end he managed to recover some 700 marks which he kept for himself and used to pay someone who smuggled him across the border without a passport.

Had I been in possession of my passport at that time I would have been in Palestine by December 1939: A former colleague of my brother's at the Rothschild hospital in Vienna, a Dr. Nelly Blum, introduced me to a cousin of hers, a Mrs. Hirsch who worked at the Palestine Office. The lady took me to the "Hechalutz" office which was just organising a transport to Palestine. Unfortunately I could only produce a photostat copy of my passport and that was unacceptable. The transport with Mrs. Hirsch safely arrived at its destination. At any rate, it was thanks to those two ladies that I made contact with the "Hechalutz".

In the end I got my passport back and resumed the search for an escape route. Another opportunity turned up for crossing into Yugoslavia illegally and I decided to try my luck once more, despite the experience of the earlier attempt. Fortunately I withdrew at the last moment. I had an uneasy feeling and pleaded footsoreness. It was a wise decision, and a lucky one. The 12 people involved passed both German and Yugoslav frontier posts only to be arrested a short distance into Yugoslavia. They were frogmarched back and finished up in a concentration camp.

Ever since the "Anschluss" I had found it impossible to obtain a visa. Now that the war had started it was altogether out of the question of gaining entry into any country legally. So I again turned to the "Hechalutz" in the hope that they might help me to get to my brother in Palestine. Earlier on I had tried to get on to one of the transports on several occasions, but officially they only took people under 35—later under 45—although some people over that age seemed to have made it somehow. Having found it impossible to join my family in Yugoslavia early in 1939 when they were still there I had tried for Palestine without success. Another plan of emigrating to Uruguay fell through at about that time, although the Uruguayan consul in Zagreb had given my wife a definite promise. My brother had made some futile efforts to obtain a "capitalist's" certificate with which I could have entered Palestine. After the abortive Yugoslav venture the one remaining hope of escape now was an illegal journey to Palestine. But the "Hechalutz" wanted 2000 marks and this I did not possess. Deportation to Poland threatened and two transports of 2000 people each had left Vienna already. It might be my turn any day.

Among the people who had been sharing my flat for the last year or so was a gentleman by name of Dr. Edel. One day he suggested that we should try for Palestine together. He was willing to raise the money for me, but in the event I managed to borrow it from elsewhere. Dr. Edel was a chemist. He hoped to produce chemicals in Palestine and I was to be his assistant and to "repay him out of the proceeds of that joint venture while my brother would no doubt put me up once we got there". On such flimsy grounds were future plans laid!

I went back to the "Hechalutz" office in early October. The "Hechalutz" was a Zionist organisation which trained young people in agriculture and various trades in order to prepare them for immigration and integration into the Jewish homeland. They also taught them Hebrew. The organisation was supervised by the Palestine Office, but the latter would only deal with applicants who held legal immigration certificates and opposed (or at least pretended to refuse to support) any attempts at illegal immigration into Palestine.

The people running the "Hechalutz" were all youngsters. The movement was headed by a handsome and serious minded young fellow by name of Ehud Überall who organised the difficult task without

wasting words. The treasurer was Emil Schächter and his brother
Rudolf was the secretary. A smart and matter-of-fact youth by name
of Goldenbaum dealt with problems which involved the mammoth
task of procuring 1200 passports and the various vital endorsements
such as Slovakian transit visas and some ostensible visa for the puta-
tive final destination. The latter was to be provided by the Bolivian or
Paraguayan consulate. After a long wait in the corridors of the
"Hechalutz" I was finally admitted. Emil Schächter instructed me to
produce my passport within the hour. I could then be included in a
transport which was due to leave within the week. I took a taxi home
to fetch Dr. Edel and we returned at once with our passports and the
money. When everything was completed we congratulated each other
as if we had won the jackpot, but Schächter remarked: "If this were a
legal journey, certificates and all, you might be right to rejoice!"

I had frequent occasion to recall these words, for the journey
claimed many victims in Bratislava, down the Danube, on the oceans,
on the Greek islands where we dropped anchor, in Haifa, on the way
to Mauritius and on the island of Mauritius itself, where the harvest
among the weary and emaciated travellers, now exposed to tropical
diseases in a dilapidated colonial prison, was particularly rich.

Small groups were to be dispatched at two-day intervals. Dr. Edel
and I asked to be included in the same group. The journey did not start
within the week as expected but was postponed several times. It was a
time of worry and frustration. My luggage comprised three large suitcases and had been sent off via Yugoslavia and Trieste long before the
abortive Yugoslav venture. These suitcases eventually arrived at my
brother's flat in Haifa.

Every participant pledged himself to obey the transport leader's instructions to the letter. All correspondence referring to the transport
was forbidden. This is the reason why my letters from Bratislava may
have seemed confused and difficult to interpret. They had to remain
cool and impersonal, though my heart was full of longing. The leaders
accepted no responsibility for actually getting us to Palestine, nor
could they guarantee the safety of our possessions or indeed our survival. The journey itself was expected to take about three to four
weeks. The gross weight of luggage was not to exceed 10 kilos. The
suitcase should preferably be old and cheap looking—it was going to
be dumped into the sea on arrival, anyway. The items taken were only
to be those considered essential for a relatively short journey. The
purchase of these proved most difficult. Coupons were required for

most items and these were only issued in exceptional cases. One
could not buy a rucksack; clothes, underwear and shoe coupons were
available to "Aryans" only. But even with coupons, the goods available in the shops were generally of very poor quality. The Nazis had
taken over and bankrupted the Jewish shops long ago. I was therefore
not at all well equipped and this presently caused a great deal of
hardship.

Those of the youngsters who had passed their Hechalutz ("Hach-
sharah") training contributed to the cost whatever they could afford,
which may have been very little or even nothing at all, while the
major contributions came from the older people.

As we were waiting for departure the ever present threat of deportation to Poland hung over our heads and presented the greatest worry.
Once I was actually instructed to report to the Aspang railway station
for deportation within 48 hours. In this most desperate situation the
"Hechalutz" gave me a document which stated that I was included in a
transport to Palestine and with it I applied to be struck off the Nazis'
list for "resettlement". This was rejected out of hand on the grounds
that an illegal journey "could not be seriously considered to be a
genuine emigration scheme". I asked for eight days' postponement.
Two days later I learned that this had also been refused. I produced a
fresh document from the Hechalutz stating that their transport would
leave within the week. In the event the authorities relented and ruled
that those who were about to leave on a Palestine transport were to be
exempt from deportation to Poland. The next day brought a renewed
instruction to report at the station for "resettlement", but this had been
sent in error—or maybe it was another little joke in the Nazis' cat-
and-mouse game. These were the days when I went into hiding with at
an acquaintance's of Dr. Edel's and went out only when absolutely essential business forced me to do so. I shall always be indebted to Dr.
Edel and Dr. Blum whose constant encouragement saved me from a
breakdown. Dr. Edel himself kept me company and never left while I
was in hiding. On November 26th he was called for departure to
Palestine. The actual destination, of course, was not put in writing,
only the one which had been entered into the passport as the "final"
visa. We had hoped to travel together, but I had to stay behind.

Next day I went to the Hechalutz office. The staff had mostly gone
and the office was being wound up. The passport specialist Goldenbaum told me that the contingent was complete and that the Gestapo
had refused to supply any more trucks for the trip to Bratislava, but

that I might be included in the emigration scheme of "Rothgasse" which was being set up by a Mr. Storfer. If I didn't like it I could have my 2000 marks back. With the threat of deportation hanging over me I went to complain to Dr. Rothenberg, the head of the Palestine office and found others there who were in the same predicament He promised to try and help, although it was not really his business. At last I received a message on November 30th instructing me to report to the Eastern Railway Station at 6 a.m. the next morning.

As Dr. Edel was leaving he refused to say good-bye since we were sure to meet again in Bratislava. He even pretended to envy me for being spared the discomfort of having to stay in barns overnight. I never saw him again. As soon as he had reached Bratislava he was transferred to the Danube steamer "Uranus" together with 800 other people. The ship stayed in the port of Bratislava for 20 days, left in mid-December, got stuck in the iced-up river at Kladovo and the travellers never got any further. What eventually happened to them is not known, though it is certain that the Germans caught up with them when they invaded the Balkans. They have never, to the best of my knowledge, been heard of again.

Vienna 1936, with Henny Schück (future daughter-in-law)

2. Bratislava

Quite a different situation arose in Bratislava. An entirely new way of life was imposed upon us and we had to adjust accordingly. It took some time before one became accustomed to living in a large community which was closely packed together, to sleeping on the floor, eating out of mess tins and lacking all privacy. Even on the toilet one was left undisturbed for scarcely a minute, for somebody was sure to hammer at the door the moment one had got in.

We had left Vienna at 7 p.m. and had had the coaches entirely to ourselves. A blond youth by name of Chaskel Preiss was appointed leader of our group of 70 people which was made up of men, women and children. Scarcely anybody knew anyone else, but I happened to see one Stiasny who had been a grocer, and Herschele Landauer who had been a singer in a Russian Cabaret and who had also occasionally served as a cantor in a synagogue. The two had been comrades in misfortune during the earlier Yugoslav debacle.

When we reached the frontier we received a special farewell from our homeland—we were made to stand in the driving rain for hours. My luggage consisted of an old travelling case, a small rucksack and two blankets, one of which my younger boy had been using in scout camp in the old days. The second blanket was an old divan cover. Slovak customs and passport control had been done on the train and we arrived at the capital at 1 a.m. The passports were impounded by the police. Buses awaited us at the station, each one with two "Hlinka guards", the police of the Slovak puppet government. We were taken to the "Slobodarna" or bachelors' home, a modern building which had been built for the city of Bratislava in the days of President Masaryk. It had five floors, but no lift, either because this had been overlooked by the architect or because bachelors are not supposed to need one.

There were single rooms, but they were not for us. The transport leaders had hired a large hall which used to be the lounge, as well as the basement and a communal room on the fifth floor. The women were accommodated separately in another part of the building and they were closely guarded by Hlinka men.

I spent the first night in a vestibule behind the lounge. This room served as a passageway to the washroom and to the lavatory, with another door leading to the office. There was insufficient room to lie down, so I sat on my suitcase till six in the morning, wet through. The lounge itself was packed with 120 people who shared about 60 mattresses which had been pushed together with only narrow gangways between them and these were choked with luggage. The mattresses appeared to be rejects from a babies' home, they were soiled and had obviously never had the benefit of rubber sheets. Moreover, they were torn and their entrails protruded through large gashes in the covers. They were constantly trodden upon and presently took on the appearance of doormats. During the day they were piled atop of one another in order to afford more space.

The air was thick with dust, sweat and tobacco smoke. The room was centrally heated and was dry and hot. As people got up in the morning a din arose which did not subside until lights-out at 10 p.m. Not that people were all that noisy, but the steady hum was not unlike that of a busy railway station concourse. We awaited further developments, never imagining that our departure from Bratislava could be much delayed. In the event nine months were to pass before we resumed our journey.

The mark of persecution was engraved upon the faces of the older people. The Nazis had been harassing them for the last 20 months, they had been robbed, expropriated and turned out of their homes. Many had been in concentration camps. They would squat upon the dirty mattresses with dim eyes and hollow cheeks, thinking of their wives and children and their brothers and sisters in far-away countries. They had been scattered by the storm of persecution which Hitler had unleashed, but they had found a temporary sanctuary of sorts, by a great stroke of luck. Austria had become a living hell for Jews. Their "Aryan" friends of yesteryear looked away lest they were seen associating with Jews and reported the Gestapo. Few of them had remained steadfast in the face of the terror. One's home was no longer one's castle—a knock at the door and one might be taken in what was euphemistically called "protective custody", but which really meant unspeakable torture or even death.

On the day following our arrival I moved into the lounge. The constant drone persisted throughout the day. During the night that followed I slept peacefully; for the first time in 20 months there was no fear of an ominous knock at the door and no likelihood of being arrested on the street, while in Vienna any civilian might challenge you in the street, ask if you were a Jew and have you arrested on the spot. Such an "arrest" was often accompanied by the seizure of the keys and a thorough "aryanisation" of one's apartment and one's shop. Although this was not exactly legal even by the standards of the new rulers, it counted for little, provided that the challenger had friends in the Nazi party who were given a share of the loot.

Food was plentiful at first, but soon the fleshpots of Bratislava, with their potatoes and occasional dumplings and gravy were to become a nostalgic memory.

The sanitary facilities were atrocious. There was just one wash basin for 120 people. In the beginning a few smart people got up at 4 a.m., but the idea soon caught on and there were long queues in front of the washroom at all hours. Of course, there was no provision for personal laundry or for cleaning the mess tins and there were only two toilets.

A few days later a contingent arrived from Prague. Most of them were well below 35. They were simply known as "the Praguers" while we were "the Viennese". In truth most of us were from neither place, having originally come from other parts of Bohemia or from Galicia. The Galicians had come to Vienna as refugees during the first world war and were now refugees for a second time. The "Praguers" differed from the "Viennese" in a number of ways, quite apart from their ages. They were generally well-organised Zionists. Some of them had escaped from Austria to Czechoslovakia after the "Anschluss", but before Hitler overran Czechoslovakia well. They were generally well fitted out since the "aryanisation" of the shops had not been as popular among the local population there as it had been in Vienna. Indeed, the Czechs had never had much love for the Germans, still less for the German fascist invaders. They showed much sympathy for those whom the Nazis persecuted and did some shopping for Jews. In Vienna such a kindness was rare and shopkeepers refused to sell to Jews either because they allowed themselves to be intimidated or because they were themselves good antisemites. Neither were the Praguers restricted in their luggage allowance and they had been able to obtain export licences for anything they wished to take along. Many of them had splendid riding boots, a fine sports suit and a rainproof mac, a big strong rucksack and two large suitcases the contents of which had been carefully chosen with due regard to the experience of earlier emigrants. Their blankets were new and they had lots of tinned food. They were an elite and the Viennese were the poor relations. Also, many of them had grown up in an atmosphere of Czech nationalism with its traditional hatred of the Habsburg Austrian Empire. This did not altogether end after 1918 and the Czech Jews were no more immune to the virus of chauvinism than those around them. Lacking, as yet, any pronounced Jewish national consciousness, they thought of themselves as Czechs and of their Viennese fellow Jews as Austrians.

The Viennese, on the other hand, were quite unorganised. They were a motley lot, some of them highly distinguished in the arts, sciences, medicine or law, others skilled artisans and most of them were hard working family men who had been uprooted, traumatised and disoriented. For the young people from Prague life had only just begun and was an exciting challenge; they had been spared the full exposure to the Nazi terror and had enjoyed the sympathy of the native population who gave them some support and protection. If the "Viennese" were somewhat undisciplined, this was scarcely surprising, bearing in mind that they had been haphazardly thrown together and that they had been driven from pillar to post. The Praguers considered themselves the cream of settlers and looked down upon the of Viennese as an undisciplined horde. Not unnaturally, this caused resentment. We had the tragicomic spectacle of an historic rerun of the friction between an arrogant master race and the quasi-colonial tribe of an empire, an empire that had been buried twenty years earlier, a spectacle with a cast of Jews from Vienna and Prague respectively and set in an overcrowded bachelors' home in Bratislava, of all places!

During the third night I began to feel the after-effects of the night which I had spent in the vestibule, wet through to the skin. A cold took hold of me and I began to cough. Bronchitis developed, an illness which had lately begun to cause me much discomfort.

The Hlinka men who were guarding us were a carbon copy of Mussolini's militia. They were named after their founder, a separatist cleric who had been agitating for Slovakia's secession during the days of the Czechoslovak republic. On his death Father Tiso assumed the leadership. The commander of the Hlinka guards was a Slovak Nazi by name of Sano Mach. There were also German Nazis in the Hlinka guard who had been recruited from their own ethnic minority. They staged "actions" against Slovak Jews and particularly enjoyed wrecking synagogues. However, there was constant friction between them and the Slovaks in the guards. The Germans came out on top when Mach was removed from command. To be fair, the Hlinka men opposed the more violent excesses against the Jews and also resented the antisemitic legislation which the German minority deputy Karmasin tried to push through the Slovakian puppet parliament, so the Germans did not quite have it their own way with their more extreme demands for a while. Such antisemitic laws as were passed at the time were relatively mild, even though antisemitism was part of the Hlinka "programme". At first the "aryanisation" of Jewish firms was confined to the owner acquiring a gentile partner; the Jew then had up to three years within which to remove himself from the business altogether and he could even have his "share" paid out. Professional people like doctors, lawyers, pharmacists, bank employees and civil servants, on the other hand, were forbidden to continue in practice or to stay in their posts. Bad though this was, it was not enforced with the same brutality as in Germany or Austria. Neither did the Slovaks gloat over the plight of the Jews like the Germans and Austrians.

The commandant of the guard was a fellow called Vasina. When he arrived he was a major and he was later promoted to colonel. He had once been a corporal in the Czech army and before that a concierge in civilian life. His men were quite decent chaps who had a little compassion with us. Their sympathy increased in proportion to their intake of schnapps. On occasion they might allow an inmate an hour's leave, something that had been quite impossible in the early days. However, the Viennese had no money other than the 10 marks which they had been allowed to take out, and even these 10 marks had been impounded by the transport leaders for the purchase of provisions. (There were some rumours of embezzlement and of somebody making off to America with the money, but this is a far-fetched story.)

The devotees of Bacchus were headed by big Stefan. He, too, had been a concierge in civilian life. Another was bowlegged Pavlik who was a very decent fellow. He did not accept bribes. In any case, I did not have enough money for a postage stamp to write to my wife, let alone for bribing a guard. The concierges, being, as it were, specially qualified for guard duty, stopped unauthorised persons from entering and freely allowed leave of absence, especially to reliable schnapps providers. There were constant squabbles between the police who had jurisdiction over us and the guards to whom the executive power had been delegated. The guards wanted to be recognised as the supreme authority and ignored police orders. The police retaliated by declaring their orders invalid. Whoever won, it was us who were taking the rap. When the police gave us leave the guards would give us house arrest. When the guards decided to let us out the police would refuse to issue the necessary passes. In the end a compromise was worked out. The police handed a number of blank passes to the guards and the guards started to trade them, sharing the profit with the police.

We expected to continue our journey any day, yet the departure was put off, day in, day out. We were travellers stranded in an improvised waiting room which was acquiring the attributes of permanence.

"Vychazka!" The voice was big Stefan's. Exercise! Not right outside, indeed, but in two small backyards in which the several hundred inmates of the "Slobodarna" could scarcely move. Slowly we milled round and round. It was cold and my feet became icicles. In a neighbouring enclosure some young people formed a circle and danced a hora; it was the only opportunity for them to get together. A quarter of an hour later a window would open and big Stefan would shout "Horé!" (upstairs!). This became a twice daily routine which was only cancelled when the colonel or big Stefan were drunk. "Exercise" was the only time when one could get away from the dust, from the smoke and from the stench of the lounge.

In the lounge there was not a moment's peace. "Schaner!" shouted big Stefan. He was the transport leader and the colonel wanted to see him. Excitement, rumours and expectations of an imminent departure being discussed. Schaner returned. Nothing. The tension ebbed away and gave way to the resumption of the usual infernal din.

People started telling their stories as they squatted on the dirty mattresses. They related how they had had to queue in front of the emigration office in the Prinz Eugenstrasse in order to obtain a passport and a certificate which confirmed that they did not owe any taxes. The tax certificate was valid for a maximum of two months and would often expire before departure, so that they had to start queuing all over again, from six in the morning till five in the afternoon. Some started queuing in front of the Rothschild Palais well before midnight. Gangs of Nazis would come along and "conscript" them to wash their cars, clean their jackboots or scrub the pavement. This was followed by goose-stepping broom-and-bucket parades, to the accompaniment of the jeering taunts of a mocking crowd of spectators. Queuing in the Prinz Eugenstrasse was dangerous but unavoidable. People were frequently beaten up and many retained permanent mementos of the occasion. One man told us: "They came at night, hauled us out of bed, beat me, the wife and the children, broke up the furniture and threw the pieces out of the window." Each story seemed to surpass the preceding one in sordid detail. Had these stories been passed on in Vienna the victims would have been arrested for "spreading tales of horror" and they might well have ended up in a concentration camp. Their ashes might eventually be returned to the family together with a bill for the transport costs and a label on the urn with the inscription: "Shot while trying to escape".

After supper people would form small groups. Card players gathered together, chess boards appeared, but the players found it hard to concentrate amid the din and the incessant milling of the crowd around them. Singers and harmonica players would come together in a small antechamber, first and foremost of them Herschele Landauer who was of Romanian origin. His nickel-framed spectacles were drooping from one side to the other, his nose was red and his clothes shabby, but he had such a beautiful voice and sang with touching gentleness, yet with such devotion and fervour that the listener was profoundly moved and greatly comforted. Herschele had a pathological persecution mania. During the abortive Yugoslav venture he had had fits of terror every time he saw a dog. Even the little pooch of the peasant who was sheltering us at the time used to terrify him. When it sniffed his trousers he would raise his leg in helpless anguish. He was equally scared of being touched by the peasant's two year old child. He was afraid of fountain pens, pencils and door knobs. When he had to open a door he would use his elbows or ask someone else to do it for him. Yet his singing was out of this world. He slept not many paces from me. His neighbour had to force him to undress at night—he would refuse to get out of his clothes in case he might have to escape from dogs. At dawn he would be found in his clothes again. He often asked me whether I thought that dog in Yugoslavia had bitten him and whether he would now get rabies. I tried to calm him down and assured him that if the dog had indeed been rabid the symptoms would have shown up long ago. Those who had known him before the "Anschluss" said that he never used to have this pathological fear of dogs.

Winter arrived early that year. It started to freeze during the first days of December. When we left Vienna we had not expected to spend more than two or three days in Bratislava. As our stay there lengthened into weeks and months and our optimism was beginning to wear thin we still refused to believe that the journey would not be resumed presently. We might have fretted less had we been told at the outset that delays and hiccups were quite likely to occur. As it was, rumour and speculation spread like wildfire. As the cold weather closed in we began to fear that the Danube might freeze over and bring all river traffic to a halt, which indeed it presently did.

A week after our arrival in the "Slobodarna" I became feverish and was transferred to a small room through the good offices of Dr. Steinhauer, a doctor from Prague. I was the second sick case. Three others presently joined us and the five of us lay on mattresses on the floor, closely packed together, with our heads and feet touching opposite walls. There was a powerful radiator in the room and it became unbearably hot. We began to argue about the setting of the radiator and in the end it was left on, while the window was opened a little.

As the days passed I was beginning to wonder whether I would ever get fit enough to resume the journey. More people arrived from Vienna in batches of 20 and 30. 800 Viennese had already been loaded onto the Danube steamer "Uranus" and had been cooped up there for three weeks. On December 16th we heard that another 200 were about to join them, some of them only quite recent arrivals, while 70 of us had been waiting to embark for over three weeks. Among those on board the "Uranus" was Dr. Edel. It was only much later that I realised how lucky I had been not to have been on that ship. It got stuck in the pack ice, the passengers were dumped ashore in Yugoslavia and Hitler caught up with many of them there. At the time it had seemed that Yugoslavia was a safe, if temporary, haven compared to Slovakia, a satellite state with an active and vociferous German minority all of whom were fanatical Nazis who ran a para-military organisation, the "Deutsche Wehr", on SS lines. Not to mention that one was constantly reminded of the proximity of the Reich just across the river.

A few days after the departure of the "Uranus" my temperature dropped, but the bronchitis persisted. We were promised the resumption of our journey soon after Christmas. The original transport leaders had left on the "Uranus" and a decent—if somewhat limited— young fellow had been put in charge. He needed a deputy who could speak Slovak and who was reasonably presentable. We elected a tall chap with brown riding boots who had assumed the title of "chief engineer" and who turned out to be no smarter than his boss, yet just as arrogant and conceited. He and the colonel of the guards became great pals and he moved freely about the town during the day. His friendship was available, at a price, and he became known as "Riding

Boots". In truth, there was no need for our representative to come and go at all hours of the day, but the "leaders" claimed that they had to attend conferences at a Slovak travel agency concerning our departure. The results of those conferences, if indeed they ever took place, were never made known on the grounds that secrecy was essential. It soon transpired that the "leader" spent much time in female company at a café near the travel agency. The real and effective leader was Goldenberg who lived in a nearby hotel and who would drive up to the "Slobodarna" occasionally. He claimed that he had to stay at a place from where he could make international telephone calls and this sounded plausible. There was also a certain Rabl with him who presently found alternative accommodation in town.

Christmas came and went and it became obvious that we would have to wait till well into the new year, but we were getting accustomed to delay. In this organisation nothing ever seemed to click. Early January brought no signs of a move. In mid-January Goldenberg gave a pep talk, assuring us that the Zionist organisation and "Rothgasse" were behind us and he exhorted us "to remain true to ourselves and to Vienna". This caused an outburst of sardonic laughter and uncomplimentary expletives. "Rothgasse" had been Storfer's enterprise. Its actual name was "Overseas Transports". Goldenberg promised that we would leave within ten days. Storfer was a Jew, but he had the ear of the Gestapo because he was organising the departure of Jews. We were not altogether certain whether he was exclusively motivated by an altruistic concern for the suffering of his people.

Goldenberg's expressed wish that we "remain true to Vienna" was almost literally fulfilled during the months that followed, for we were repeatedly threatened with being returned there. What Goldenberg had meant that we should keep ourselves apart from the Praguers and preserve an identity which some of us did not possess in the first place, while the rest of us had no particular reason to be reminded of Vienna, still less to be proud of the city. Anyway, Goldenberg's speech had little to do with Zionism and did not help promote an improved rapport between the Viennese and the Praguers.

We were told that the ship which was to have taken us from Sulina on the Danube estuary across the Black Sea had sunk—hence the delay—and that a replacement was on its way from Greece which was confidently expected to arrive any day. That winter the Danube froze over completely. Great falls of snow and an alternation of hard frosts and sunshine transformed the river into a glacier. All hope of leaving before the spring thaw had gone.

The police began to allow people to go into town for shopping under armed guard in groups of six, but on one's return one had to prove that some purchases had in fact been made; presently they issued half-day permits and this was good business for the guards as well as for "Riding Boots" who was not averse to accepting consideration in cash or in kind, but it did not give me much of a chance, for I had nothing with which to bribe these people. Aggravated by the dry, dusty and smoke-polluted atmosphere my cough became steadily worse and I begged Drs. Steinhauer, Lederer and Kummermann to help me get out for a breath of fresh air. These doctors had come from Prague. The Viennese had only one doctor, a Dr. Wagner who had been a chief medical officer in the ambulance service. He had been aboard the "Uranus" where he had fallen sick himself and from whence he had been transferred to the Jewish hospital in town. In his absence the doctors from Prague looked after the Viennese as well. Later on more doctors arrived from Vienna These were allocated to the "Patronka", another refugee hostel which contained only Viennese.

Eventually Dr. Steinhauer obtained a permit for me without having to bribe a guard. Bowlegged Pavlik very kindly took me to Fochgasse 11 where a Mrs. Friedmann lived. I had a message for her from her sister, the wife of Dr. Buxbaum who had been a tenant of my elder son's mother-in-law. Mrs. Friedmann lived in a pleasant modern house, together with her 15 year old daughter and her 14 year old son. Their part of the apartment consisted of two rooms with bath and was quite elegant. Another room had been let to a young lady who had come from the provinces in the hope of finding an opportunity for emigration. Mrs. Friedmann gave me a large jar of apricot jam, some cake and 10 Slovak crowns. It was quite embarrassing for me to accept money from strangers for the first time in my life. On hearing me describe the conditions in the "Slobodarna" Mrs. Friedmann promised to obtain half-day permits for me, so that my cough should have a chance to get better. That cost 40 crowns. The good people of Bratislava were more helpful and compassionate than most people I had come across either before or since.

In order to prove that I had "bought something" I purchased a pound of apples which I shared with my fellow inmates. The first leave lasted for an hour and a half, but I had to walk briskly. Unaccustomed to exercise as I was after having been cooped up for two months I was stiff and suffered from muscular pains for days.

One night in the small hours some 400 out of the 500 people in the "Slobodarna" were struck by diarrhoea. Appalling scenes occurred around the toilet, with hundreds demanding access at once. A few days later we read in the newspapers that the outbreak of diarrhoea had been due to food poisoning caused by some tainted cocoa that we had been given the evening before. A police investigation followed and it was rumoured that one of the employees of the outside caterers who were running the canteen had played a practical joke on us by putting cascara into the cocoa.

Now and again people would give talks in the evening. We began to miss Herschele's singing. He had been among those who had been transferred to the "Uranus" which had got stuck at Kladovo and was awaiting the spring thaw.

After numerous arguments with "Riding Boots", for whose receptive pocket I had been a dead loss, Mrs. Friedmann obtained a pass which entitled me to go out every other afternoon for three weeks. Mrs. Friedmann was a pious Jewish woman motivated by compassion and by a genuine desire to help people without expecting any favours in return. I often visited her. She would give me breakfast in the morning and tea in the afternoon. Then she would leave to let me enjoy the restful comfort of her home, a most welcome change from the noise and confusion of the "Slobodarna". I would enjoy the luxury of a hot bath, lie down on the divan in the parlour and recall old times. Eventually I would leave and return by way of the Danube embankment.

The snow fall had been the heaviest on record for many years. The ice was cracking and huge floes were piling up on the Danube. The combined effect of the midday sun and the hard night frosts cemented them ever more tightly together. We were told that we would leave as soon as a navigable channel opened up.

A few days later the colonel gave permission for groups of 25 people to go on outings to the countryside under guard. I went quite frequently. Once my right ear got frostbitten. We entered an inn where the guardsman bought me a glass of schnapps out of his own pocket, for I had no money on me. Although these guardsmen wore a uniform resembling that of the SS, some of them behaved like human beings. On one occasion a guardsman even stood up for us when we were attacked by a gang of Nazis. The bullies produced their party cards and the matter was reported to the commandant. We never saw the guardsman again.

I budgeted carefully with Mrs. Friedmann's 10 crowns and was occasionally able to visit a little café where I looked at the newspapers. The news was bad. They came from German sources, of course, but the reports of German victories were depressingly true. After every fresh Nazi conquest the villas of the German community flew the Nazi flag, a white circle carrying a red double cross on a blue background. It was so obviously like the Nazi emblem that the locals were none too keen on it, despite all the pressure exerted upon them to display enthusiasm.

A few weeks later Goldenberg was recalled to Vienna. He was replaced by one Rottenstreich who had been the secretary of the Palestine office until then. He was to liaise with the Slovak Jewish community and with the Joint Jewish Relief Committee and it was his job to ensure that the cost of our board and lodging was met. The situation frequently became critical, but this was not mentioned at the time in order to avoid a panic. A daily bulletin published instructions from the transport leaders and from the colonel. Rottenstreich gave numerous addresses. He was a good speaker, but when one thought about what he said it was little more than a repetition of promises with slight variations. The man was trying hard to keep up morale.

My cough got worse and became chronic. While the outings refreshed me, the intense cold also caused considerable problems. My light overcoat afforded little protection against a temperature of 15 to 20 degrees of frost. Such a coat might have been fine for a Mediterranean winter, but in this climate it was virtually useless. Towards the end of March I became feverish again and was moved to the sickroom which had been equipped with iron bedsteads. The mattresses there were even filthier than those in the great hall, but Drs. Lederer and Kummermann looked after me most conscientiously.

Dr. Lederer told me that Dr. Löwy, the radiologist from the Jewish hospital had been enquiring after me and that Dr. Blum from the Rothschild hospital in Vienna had spoken to him. When Dr. Löwy heard that I was ill he wanted to give me a thorough examination. I took a bus to the hospital and was admitted at once. They put me in an emergency ward and I had a proper bed, white sheets and a clean mattress! I ran a temperature of 101, but I was in paradise. This time I had been lucky indeed. I stayed in hospital for nearly two months and got to know a number of patients as well as the very efficient doctors. The chief medical officer was Dr. Weiss and his assistant was Dr. Feher. Dr. Löwy visited me every day and constantly enquired after my needs. He made sure that I always had fresh fruit and a piece of cake and when he noticed that I had no slippers or warm socks he brought me some at once. His kindness gave me comfort and strength, my temperature dropped and I was allowed to get up and use the reading room. The hospital was modern, well equipped and tastefully furnished. I could see Castle Hill from my window with the ruins of the old castle where Hungary's kings had been crowned centuries ago. The window of the reading room, on the other hand, afforded the less edifying view of the fine villa which had been requisitioned by the German commandant. Uniformed Nazis were constantly strutting in and out.

As May approached I was able to use the small garden which belonged to the hospital. I met Dr. Werner who at that time happened to be a hospital patient himself. He was a good friend to me, especially when I suffered a relapse and ran a temperature again. At that time I was allowed up for only a little while at lunchtime. There was also Dr. Thalheim, a one-time assistant of Prof. Tandler's and a little boy by name of Heinzi Tichler who had an ear infection. The boy had been given a ludo set and we used to play every day, which helped to keep us cheerful.

Most of the patients were from Bratislava and surrounding areas. Several people died while I was there, among them a fellow refugee whose face had seemed vaguely familiar when he was brought in. He was put next to me, but I was sent out of the ward. He died from heart disease shortly after admission. I learned at the funeral that his name was Sommer and I suddenly remembered where I had seen him before. One of the apartments in the house next to us in Vienna was inhabited by Herr Hans Reischl, a senior design engineer of a well-known battery manufacturing company. He had married our elder son's governess Lisa many years ago. Hans and Lisa had both remained loyal friends and had repeatedly taken great risks helping me and other Jewish people whenever they could. One day Lisa knocked at my door. Sommer and his wife were at their apartment and she asked me if I could help them find a way of getting to Palestine. I gave them the address of the Hechalutz and of Storfer at the Rothgasse. We went down the Burggasse and the Ringstrasse together and I soon realised that the Sommers were exceptionally fine people. He was a good looking ex-army officer who had had to leave the service

because of heart trouble. His wife was a gentile, but they were
devoted to each other. They had no children. They had been in Bratislava for some time, but I had never met them again because they had
been quartered at the "Patronka" which was the other refugee place in
town. When Mrs. Sommer returned from the funeral she took poison
and died at once. It was then that I remembered her saying that neither
of them could face life without the other. If only I had remembered in
time!

One day I was called into the reading room. A distinguished looking gentleman with a Goethe head was waiting for me. He introduced
himself as Maximilian Krafft. He was a friend of a relative of a Mr.
Oscar Pollak of Maribor (Yugoslavia). My brother had written to Mr.
Pollak asking whether his (Pollak's) relatives in Bratislava could do
anything for me. The obvious friendliness of Mr. Krafft impressed me
deeply. In reply to the question of how he could be of assistance I
asked him whether it could be arranged for me to stay at somebody's
private home after my discharge from hospital until such time as I was
able to leave Bratislava, having learned that while I had been sick, all
the Viennese from the "Slobodarna" had been transferred to the
"Patronka" and that the food had become much worse. In such circumstances the chances of a successful convalescence would have
been minimal. Mr. Krafft promised to cover the cost of any leave passes (one crown per day) and offered to help out with a little extra
money. A few days later he returned with his wife and arranged that I
should come to them for dinner four times a week. They also introduced me to Mr. and Mrs. Bondy who offered hospitality for the other
three days. These wonderful people not only built up my physical
strength with nourishing meals but gave me a great deal of much
needed moral support. It was obvious that it pleased them greatly to
be able to help and I was never made to feel an unwelcome interloper.

Although the hospital food was excellent I suffered from a lack of
appetite and was unable to eat much. I lost weight and was down to
under nine stone, two stone less than when I left Vienna, but I was
beginning to enjoy the warm spring sunshine in the garden. My
temperature had gone, although the cough persisted. I felt very weak
and I began to worry lest the transport down the Danube leave without
me, but Dr. Wagner assured me that I would be taken to the ship's
sickbay, if necessary.

I left hospital in early June. Dr. Löwy had rented a room for me
which was near the hospital. The landlord was a good and pious man

by the name of Judah Müller who lived quietly with his wife and four children. But ten days later permission to live out was rescinded and I had to move to the "Patronka".

The "Patronka" was outside the city limits, but the town was only a short bus ride away. Its name derived from the fact that it had been a munitions factory at one time. The buildings were derelict. I walked through the gate and past the porter's lodge (now occupied by a couple of Hlinka guards) and found myself in a vast yard. An evil smelling stream ran through the compound. The old factory buildings were dotted around some freshly dug fields on which volunteers worked for a daily wage of 8 crowns. The sleeping quarters were cavernous factory halls, each of them containing about a hundred straw palliasses on wooden bunks. Most of the windows were broken and the roof leaked. Each hall had a tiny iron stove. People had suffered terribly from the cold during the winter, but during the summer the "Patronka" had one advantage over the "Slobodarna": There was plenty of fresh air. Moreover, one was free to move within the compound.

When I moved in the guardsman on duty was one Novak who was a decent fellow. He took turns with bowlegged Pavlik. The refugees' leader was Dr. Merdinger and later on Dr. Neumann, with whom I got on very well. On payment of 10 crowns I obtained ten days' leave at once and was permitted to move around town freely between the hours of 8 a.m. and 7 p.m., but leave was stopped for our own protection whenever the Germans were on the rampage and attacked Jewish shops, looted homes, vandalised the synagogue and beat people up. When walking into town I usually went by way of the lovely Stefanik Nature Park which lies on a hill and is well laid out with footpaths. I would reach it within 20 minutes and often rested on a bench to read one of the books which the Kraffts had lent me. So I reached the town in easy stages. I was still weak because the cough continued to torment me day and night. I would arrive at the Kraffts about midday, but if it happened to be one of the days when the Bondys were expecting me I would take a tram from the park. On arrival a hot bath and a house coat were always ready for me. The apartments were in modern blocks of flats with the benefit of an unlimited supply of hot water. Occasionally I would take a bus straight from the "Patronka".

I also looked up Mrs. Friedmann again from time to time, but not too often, lest I embarrass her. On other occasions I would sit in a small park in front of the theatre or along the banks of the Danube, but the view into Austria across the river upset me and I never stayed there long.

I often stopped to admire the beautiful baroque architecture of the town, buildings such as St. Michael's gate and the charming narrow streets with their low houses which were many centuries old. The small provincial town had become a flourishing city of 130,000 inhabitants during the time of the Czechoslovak republic. Now it had degenerated to the status of the capital of an insignificant Nazi puppet state. The Slovak leaders had betrayed their Czech brethren and were now beginning to feel the iron heel of German oppression themselves. The well appointed modern blocks of flats in the centre and the pleasant suburban villas had been requisitioned by Germans from all over the region and the Germans were also taking over such Jewish property as had initially been "aryanised" by the local fascists. The town itself was no longer known as Bratislava; it reverted to Preßburg, its German name in the Austro-Hungarian empire.

Dr. Löwy would ask me for tea now and again. He still lived in the charming villa on a hill which afforded a magnificent view of the town, of Castle Hill and of the river. His wife was a beautiful blonde and they had a strapping boy aged five. The villa was tastefully furnished, but the Löwys were well aware that their days there were numbered. They often pressed me to accept money which I did with the greatest reluctance and only because there was no other way for me to buy essentials such as soap, stamps and writing paper. On two occasions I received 200 crowns from Dr. Bauer and Mr. Rosenblatt, who had been old friends in Zagreb, Yugoslavia. Some afternoons I went to a roadside inn run by a Czech named Klepac. The inn was to the east of the town and the way there led through a beautiful wooded valley. Sometimes the Kraffts and I would have dinner there of a Sunday.

I met a few very nice people at the "Patronka", including a Mr. Abend and Dr. and Mrs. Heller. I avoided unattached women and generally kept myself to myself, except when I was with the Kraffts, the Bondys or the Löwys, but I had an occasional game of rummy with Dr. and Mrs. Wagner or spent an afternoon with an ex-barrister whom I had met while in hospital.

Occasionally Rottenstreich would visit the "Patronka", usually of an evening, when he made speeches intended to boost morale. Rumours of impending departure would be followed by disappointment and some people gave up all hope of ever leaving Bratislava. It was rumoured that the "Patronka" camp was to be liquidated and that we were about to be billeted on hospitality to places out of town. All leave was stopped. It was the end of June and we felt that if the journey were ever to be resumed it would have to be soon.

The Slovak puppet premier Monsignor Tiso was called to Berlin. On his return the political climate shifted ominously and the Nazi extremists among the German minority became totally unrestrained. The commander of the Hlinka guards was kicked upstairs and became "Home Secretary" while the Guards and the "Deutsche Wehr" who had been jealous rivals for so long began to fraternise. A fresh outburst of antisemitic violence flared up, the windows of Jewish shops were smashed and the stock looted. Jews were barred from cafés and from public places. The woodlands and the shady parts of the "Patronka" were declared out of bounds and all manner of chicanery made life more and more difficult. The friendly attitude of the guards was changing and the transport leaders were under mounting pressure to get us out of Slovakia. Nothing, of course, would have pleased us better than to be on our way.

One of the nastiest guardsmen was one Flautner, who was believed to be a German liaison officer. He habitually used filthy and obscene language. Twice he ordered us to pack and to hurry up, lest the coaches taking us back to Germany be kept waiting. We were terrified. Eventually the refugee committee secured a temporary reprieve and the deadline was extended. This cat-and-mouse game went on for several weeks. The luggage had to be ready for instant departure and nobody knew whether for emigration or for deportation to an unknown destination. Assurances from our leaders alternated with threats from the guards. The food was getting rapidly worse, despite the fact that there was as yet no shortage, but most people had no money to buy extras and I recalled with nostalgia the splendid sausages and the luscious fruit that I had enjoyed not so very long ago. I had already taken my leave from the friends in town on two occasions. At the Kraffts, who had done so much for me, tears were streaming down my face—tears of joy at the anticipated departure mixed with tears of sorrow at losing such wonderful friends whom I would surely never see again and who had given me courage when all hope seemed to have gone. Both times I returned and was welcomed back with open arms. The food at the "Patronka" had become awful and it was a great boon to be a guest at the table of friends in town. When the Bondys went on holiday in August they set up a 150 crown credit account at a local delicatessen shop for me, so that I could supplement my rations.

The newspapers, led by the German "Grenzbote", vied with each other in antisemitic incitement. With our experience of Nazi brutalities our apprehensions increased accordingly. On the 22nd of August Rottenstreich came to tell us that the Viennese and the Praguers from the "Slobodarna" were to leave within two days. On the 24th he reappeared, saying that there was room for only 200 people since 500 more were due in Bratislava from Danzig and they had to be accommodated on the Danube steamer "Helios" which was coming down the river from Vienna. The remaining 400 Viennese were to follow in her sister ship "Uranus" two days later. Tempers boiled over. Nobody seemed to believe that we were really about to leave, even when the ships actually entered the harbour. Tension grew and everybody wanted to know who was to he among the first 200. Colonel Vasena declared that anybody who made trouble would be put in prison. He stated that the list was being compiled by the police and that no appeal was possible, but it was probably the transport leaders who were saddled with this invidious task.

Karl Lenk c 1920

Karl Lenk c 1914

3. "Helios"

August 26th. We were taken to the harbour in buses and were about to embark on the "Helios", one of the fleet of the Danube Steamship Company. Her sister ship, the "Uranus" had anchored alongside. Both were of a good size. They used to take passengers on pleasure cruises down to the estuary and to the Romanian Black Sea ports. Two smaller ships, the "Melk" and the "Schönbrunn" were there as well, having brought more "Praguers" and some "Berliners" down from Vienna.

Slovak customs men thoroughly searched the luggage. Guardsman Flautner kicked my bag and pushed me in the ribs shouting: "Get out with that lousy stuff!" My people had been hard working and had lived in Austria for generations, but no matter. I said nothing, glad to leave the accursed former homeland at last.

There were 535 "Danzigers" on the "Helios" already. They had gone aboard the night before, had made themselves comfortable and were not keen to share the accommodation with further arrivals. There was some pushing and shoving and one man who had had his wife and child with him fell off the gangway and was drowned. The ship stayed in the winter harbour until the 3rd of September because the police did not want us near the town centre where the locals would stare at us from the jetty. That day a further 350 Praguers from the "Slobodarna" joined us; like the Viennese from the "Patronka" they had been in Bratislava for nine months. There were 1095 men, women and children aboard now, but officially there was cabin space for only 250. The Danzigers had 50 children with them, as well as a larger number of old people than any other group. There were people from every walk of life, including some whom the Gestapo wanted deported. There was no cohesion among them and those who had boarded first thought that they were entitled to special privileges. It took a little while before the "Haganah" police force which the Praguers had organised was able to establish some kind of order.

The crew consisted of Germans and Austrians. They were not altogether averse to being on leave from the fatherland for a while and, except for the robber barons who ran the canteen, they behaved correctly. The ships were not, of course, going down the river for our benefit. They were to pick up "Volksdeutsche" from Russian-occupied Bessarabia and our transportation on the downstream leg just helped to pay for what was a strictly commercial transaction.

People were bedding down wherever they could—in the dining room, in the gangways or on deck, spreading their blankets on the floor. It took a couple of days before some order was established and before people got used to queuing for food and for the ablutions. Guards were posted in front of the drinking water taps. The Praguers had trained a "Haganah" police force in secret and presently recruited some more young men from the Viennese and from the Danzigers to add to their number. This police force of ours quickly became highly efficient.

For the first two nights I slept in a cabin for two which I shared with five others, two in each bunk and two on the floor. The cabins were later taken over by the women and I moved to a communal cabin which normally served as the crew's quarters. It was reasonably comfortable there, but the air was thick. The food was not too bad at first, but soon deteriorated. No matter. The weather was fine and we were on our way. Our hearts lifted with hope as the overcrowded vessel made its way downstream. The "Uranus" was about half an hour ahead. We passed the picturesque towns of Komorom and Gran which were situated on a broad plain amid vineyards and woods. Gran is on a river bend and its magnificent bishop's palace stands on top of a steep rock, obviously at one time the home of a warlike cleric. We passed Waitzen and reached majestic Budapest with its handsome bridges and ancient palaces. There we stopped for a few hours. It was evening and the police prevented the inquisitive crowd from approaching too closely. Next day we passed Mohacs and entered Yugoslavia. The landscape was flat and the banks were covered with shrubbery. We could see the military barracks of the garrison town of Novi Sad and passed Belgrade. On the following day we reached the "Iron Gate". A magnificent spectacle opened before us. Wide lakes alternated with bends and narrow rapids until we got to Kladovo where some people were waving from the river bank. They were members of the contingent that had left Bratislava during the winter. They had got stranded there and Dr. Edel may well have been among them. How we had envied them when they were leaving, not knowing when it would be our turn, still less imagining that this would take nine months! What would be the fate of those poor souls now? A sombre mood overtook us. The "Uranus", now ahead of us, had dumped these unfortunate people and had returned upstream. Now she was carrying the remaining Viennese from the "Patronka" as well as some who had arrived from Vienna more recently. There were "only" 950 aboard and they were a little less overcrowded than the "Helios", where the jostling never ceased.

Next morning we arrived at the Bulgarian port of Rustchuk. As we entered the harbour we saw a tiny dirty grey paddle steamer with a rusty chimney. It was the "Pencho" which had left Bratislava three months earlier with a load of 300 Slovak Zionists. They had come a distance which any ordinary river boat would have covered in three days. They were lining the railings, their faces haggard and emaciated. The vessel listed dangerously as they crowded onto the starboard side and implored us to pick them up or, at least to give them some food. They were riding at anchor in the international zone of the river, having been forbidden to approach either the Romanian or the Bulgarian bank. They were therefore unable to obtain food and drinking water. The boat had left Bratislava without a transit visa and the leaders had hoped to obtain those locally as necessary. At times they had been obliged to wait for weeks and the provisions which were to have lasted them until they reached Palestine had given out. Now they faced starvation. What madness to contemplate a journey on the high seas in such an ancient coffin! But what risks were people not prepared to take in a desperate attempt to escape certain death?

All of us decided to forego a meal. The "Melk" and the "Schönbrunn" had caught up with us and they also gave up a meal to the "Pencho" people who had survived on scraps of potato peelings for the last few days. We even raised a little money. The authorities of the riparian states would not let the "Pencho" pass because of her derelict condition, but neither were they willing to give them any help, still less to offer refuge. It took a day before the food reached them.

The Balkans were in turmoil. The king of Romania had abdicated and had fled the country. The "Iron Guard", a band of local fascist thugs, had taken over. The new government would not recognise our transit visa at first and we had to stay on the Bulgarian side of the river, but two days later we were permitted to leave Rustchuk, presumably because the ships were flying the German flag, so they could not very well be prevented from passing on, all the more so since they were on an official mission to Bessarabia. This, ironically, was the one time that we enjoyed German protection, however unintended by either side! The evening before we left Rustchuk the "Pencho" people signalled in Morse code: "Take us with you!" We were forbidden to reply. Neither were we allowed to take food to them without Romanian permission and the Romanians threatened to shoot if anybody were to try to get to the "Pencho". At night we did hear shots. Four people had tried to swim across to us. Three men had been arrested on reaching the Bulgarian bank; the fourth, a girl, had disappeared and nobody knew whether she had been shot or whether she had been dragged down by the treacherous river currents. During the morning another three tried the same thing and were seen to climb up the Bulgarian bank a little later. The police promptly took them back to the "Pencho", but not before giving them something to eat. The Bulgarian officers and men also threw us food and cigarettes, although that was strictly forbidden. A man from Berlin who had died in Rustchuk was buried there. On September 9th we dropped anchor at Giurgiu and a Romanian officer took our gift of food across to the "Pencho". We sailed past her and saw the dirty, shabby and starving people at close quarters.

The Danzigers were "rich"! They had been allowed to take £1 each with them and spent recklessly on grapes and chocolates from the canteen, although they had been warned not to waste money. In the end they were barred from using the canteen altogether, whereupon they started to eat their emergency rations of tinned fruit. We thought of the "Pencho". The Danzigers were an undisciplined mob. Some behaved as if they were on a pleasure trip, others were forever squabbling.

Some of them had been wealthy people and had paid a lot of money to get away, while others had been poor and had not paid a penny. So far few of them had learned the lesson that all refugees are equal. The acid test of character is the ability to adjust to communal life. This is where moral values based upon a stable family background begin to tell.

Two girls, covered with make-up and dressed to kill were seen to sneak into the bunks of the canteen personnel. The crew were not much bothered by the Nuremberg race laws and paid the ladies with food and drink. Matrimonial quarrels and jealous altercations became common property.

Braila was the Romanian port from which oceangoing vessels

could reach the Black Sea. We arrived there at about noon of September 10th. Small and dirty houses huddled against large modern blocks; there were tramcars with tiny and filthy carriages alongside elegant automobiles, derelict wrecks, lorries, horse and dog carts, all in motley disarray. The people on the streets fitted into a scene of apparent confusion as they shared the pavements and the carriageways with squealing pigs and gaggling geese. We were able to observe it all, but we were not allowed to disembark for exercise and to stretch our legs. A number of Danzigers were found to have lice and the doctors had their hands full coping with the attendant problems. It was discovered that the Viennese had no medical stores whatever; what little there had been at the "Patronka" originally was now on board the "Uranus". This was to be put right at Tulçea, where we hoped to take on supplies when finally embarking on the ship that was to take us to Palestine.

We noticed a number of ships of the Danube flotilla and a great deal of military activity. Something big was afoot. We moved on to Galata, where we stayed for a few hours. Soldiers, barbed wire and gun emplacements were everywhere. We saw a blown-up railway bridge at the mouth of the river Pruth as well as Russian gunboats and sailors. When we got to Tulçea on September 12th we were not permitted to make fast on the jetty and dropped anchor in the middle of the river. We were waiting for our transfer to the oceangoing ship and were much worried by the warlike activities around. Rumours were rife, but there was no authentic news.

The final stages of the trip down the delta were of no scenic interest whatever. All that we could see were wide stretches of water and flat shrubland beyond, with the odd shack here and there, a few ragged people and some shaggy goats—rather a melancholy sight in a country rich in mineral and agricultural resources.

4. "Atlantic"

Three ancient semi-derelict vessels lay in the harbour. They were old tramp steamers with unpainted timber superstructures, matching to perfection the wretched natives in their miserable shacks along the river. They were Greek and had come from Piraeus. Carpenters were hammering away on deck, the Greek names were being painted out and replaced with the names "Atlantic", "Pacific", and "Milos". It was like naming a Pekinese "Nero" or a Chihuahua "Caesar", except that these ships had never been thoroughbreds. The flag of Panama was painted on the sides and fluttered from the mast. High up amidship the "Atlantic" six timber-built lavatory sheds had been knocked together. They hung over the side and more Panamanian flags were fluttering above them. A visit there was later referred to as "a trip to Panama".

Of the three ships, the "Atlantic" was the largest. She was long and narrow and very high at the bow. She was to take on people from the "Helios" and from the "Schönbrunn" while those from the "Uranus" were to embark on the "Pacific" and those from the "Melk" on the "Milos". One day Storfer, his deputy Goldner and a Greek named Afgherinos may be asked why 1850 souls were crammed into the "Atlantic" which scarcely had room for 1200. We could not know that the ship would list, take in water through the portholes and flood the engine room while we queued up for food. We were happy to get onto the biggest of the ships, unaware of her poor condition and of the living hell that awaited us. Re-embarkation started on September 14th without any of us ever setting foot on dry land.

The "Pacific" resembled a sailing yacht fitted up with a chimney. The little "Milos" had a blue chimney and was listing to starboard. The 1850 people from the "Helios and from the "Schönbrunn" were leaving their Danube steamers at noon while the passengers from the other river boats were transferred at 6 p.m. The transport leaders inspected the "Pacific" and the "Milos" but they were not allowed aboard the "Atlantic". The weather continued fine, as indeed it had been all the way down the river.

The "Atlantic" slowly approached the "Schönbrunn" and the "Schönbrunners" swarmed across. Their leaders and those from the "Helios" argued about the allocation of space. There was no captain to give orders and people were stumbling all over the place with their luggage. Everybody wanted a cabin, of course. The few cabins that existed were intended for women with children, but they were occupied by assorted couples who had decided to bed down together. People slept with whomever they fancied, married couples swapped partners, all decency was discarded, all morality abandoned. Age was no barrier and many a married woman with children somewhere on board snuggled up to boys who were scarcely out of their 'teens. There was a scramble for secluded corners, but in the end all had to pack together like sardines. It was the golden calf all over again and I was beginning to feel thoroughly ashamed of some of my fellow passengers.

An hour after the Schönbrunners had been transferred it was the turn of the people from the "Helios". Women with children boarded first, followed, in turn, by the other women, the elderly, the middle aged, and finally the young men. The luggage was brought aboard and there was chaos at the start, but presently the "Haganah" was able to create a semblance of order.

When I came aboard with my rucksack and blankets all the sleeping places in the upper regions had been taken. People were pushing their way through tight knots, shouting and cursing. Corners and gangways alike were choked with luggage. I scrambled over suitcases and bodies, and was propelled along rather than moving on my own. I reached the hold which was crammed. Vertical ladders led further down and there were a few unoccupied cabins on either side. Some three-tier bunks had been knocked together and a narrow gangway separated them from the cabins. A passage on the right led to the ablutions and to the drinking water supply; it became known as "water lane". The passage on the left led to the galley which had been occupied by Praguers and by Viennese from the "Patronka". I dragged my stuff along, descended a wooden staircase leading to the bottom of a shaft and arrived in front of a ramp which was tightly packed with tiered bunks right up to the ceiling. Men and women were huddled together in semi-darkness. I found myself in the very depths of the ship, well below the water line. The floor was covered with gravel chips which served as ballast. This space was also full of three-tiered bunks. A feeble ray of watery light penetrated down the shaft and illuminated a passage of about one-and-a-half by seven feet which ter-

minated near a broad ventilation shaft. The area was occupied by
Praguers and the only space left was the passage itself. I took the top
bunk in a corner near a ventilation shaft. This was a mistake because a
steam pipe ran along the wall and it became unbearably hot. Conden-
sation ran down the walls and rusty water dripped from the bulkheads.
There were barely eighteen inches of headroom, so I was unable to sit
up; I had to get in head first, stoop as much as possible and turn round
to face the passage. No two people could perform this exercise simultaneously since each had to "borrow" the other's space before turning
round. This was how 75 people crowded into an area of 16 by 18 foot
which, in addition, was barely six foot high.

The fist impression destroyed any illusions. The damned must have
felt something like that on entering Dante's Inferno. Women started to
cry and climbed up the stairs again; the men followed, swearing and
cursing. The sleeping quarters of galley slaves were paradise compared with the living hell of the "Atlantic". Storfer had said that the
sea journey would take no more than 10 days and I figured that I
should just be able to stand it that long, little knowing that those ten
days would stretch to ten weeks.

The ventilation shaft soon became festooned with clothing and
overcoats, so that hardly any air could reach us. The light shaft was
similarly hung with rucksacks. The faint glimmer of an oil lamp
produced an eery light, but oil was short and we had to go easy on
fuel. The area was wired for electricity, but the current was only
sporadically switched on at night. There was not a square inch which
was not trampled on, squatted on or slept on. When they were sweep-
ing up above, the dirt would drop down on our heads. We were unable
to sweep up ourselves because of the ballast chips on the floor, so we
had to pick up all the refuse manually. To complete our discomfort,
smoke from the galleys would drift down at times and make us gasp
for air.

The galley consisted of four colossal stewpots. They stood in the
open, next to the ventilation shaft The outside was boarded off with
wooden planks and a catwalk ran overhead. Dirt and dust would drop
from it at times. The luggage had to be redistributed during the first
night because there was no room on deck for the hundreds who had to
take turns standing so that others could sleep, while some were squat-
ting on rucksacks. Eventually the mountains of luggage disappeared
into the holds, accompanied by the owners' curses. When the engines
stopped electricity generation ceased and the water was off too be-

cause the pumps were power operated. The toilets could not be
flushed and a vile stench arose. Eventually anybody wanting to use
the toilets had to bring a pail of seawater which was pulled up on a
long rope.

My sleeping area was known as "the catacombs". People there
could only move around in knots like football fans at the turnstiles,
except that the eddies moved in opposite directions. Eventually traffic
rules were established: forward on the right, astern on the left.
Haganah traffic police controlled the flow. Occasionally we were
visited by people who would descend from the open decks above and
who considered moving in, but they mostly climbed up again in dismay.

By now the Schönbrunners had joined the Danzigers and the rest of
us. They were a mixed crowd of old people, families with young
children and working lads from the outer suburbs of Vienna. Storfer
had supposedly been forced by the Gestapo to include 200 convicts
who were, however, never identified and who would believe what the
Gestapo said anyway? Quite likely they were "criminals" only in the
sense that they were Jews.

There was incessant turmoil. Old people shuffled about restlessly
or were trodden on as they tried to snatch some sleep. Mothers
shouted for their children and others called for a doctor. Medical supplies were pooled and the Haganah did a great job in establishing
order, though some people refused to submit to discipline and had to
be persuaded by stronger arguments.

Romania was mobilising. Food was being requisitioned by the
army and rationing was introduced. According to Storfer there was a
food shortage in Tulçea which explained why we were running low,
even though we had paid through the nose for our supplies. The bread
had been baked using low-grade flour. It went mouldy within 24
hours. In the poor light we did not notice that at first, but the unmistakable tummy symptoms soon revealed the cause. The diet consisted
mainly of poor quality pulses which were boiled to make soup. When
these were delivered late we would miss a meal. The bread was
brought by ragged men in rowing boats; the drinking water came in
old wine casks from which it was baled out into storage tanks bucket
by bucket. When the fresh water supply gave out river water was
pumped in through filters. A number of people went down with
dysentery and they would make their way "to Panama" with grey and
distorted faces, delirious with stomach cramp. There were six

cubicles for 1860 people and one had to queue for hours. Neither was there anywhere to sit while waiting, since every square inch was occupied. Desperate cases received special consideration. The doctors supplied "letters of introduction" and the Haganah would let the patients through, but even those with priority passes had to form a long separate line and some relieved themselves over the side.

Political firebrands were starting to throw their weight about. Some were listened to good-humouredly because they were just too funny in their puffed-up self-importance, while others were simply ignored. Groups of orderlies (there was no shortage of volunteers) took on the distribution of bread and several of them doled it out as if they had paid for it. They certainly made sure that there was enough for themselves. Three days later the four kitchen units began to function. One or two of them prepared kosher food. The galleys received their supplies according to the number of people for whom they were catering. Each kitchen had a representative at the stores to make sure that they got their fair share. There were accusations of graft, but there was neither proof nor remedy. Even the Haganah was suspected—probably quite unjustly. However, after all the initial squabbling the various groups settled down under the overall leadership which mainly consisted of Praguers who were aware of similar problems on earlier Palestine transports and who had come well prepared to deal with them. They had cooking utensils, buckets, ropes, brooms and emergency lighting equipment. Storfer brought more over from Tulçea, but most of the materials were hard to come by and consequently in short supply.

During the second night there was a heavy thunderstorm. Those on deck were soaked to the skin. The elderly were sent to the "catacombs". They looked down in horror, though we did our best to accommodate them. Eventually they squatted on the stairways down which water was cascading in torrents.

There was no crew aboard as yet and some people would sleep in the engine room. The dining hall served a dormitory for the very old and they lay on the floor, packed like sardines. The stench was awful and the place soon became infested with lice. Some of these poor people were incontinent and quite incapable of looking after themselves. There was no question of them joining the scramble for buckets, of hoisting up water, or even of making it to "Panama".

The captain had disappeared. He had refused to accept responsibility for an overcrowded and unseaworthy ship and had demanded that at least 500 people be taken off. Storfer promised that a fourth ship would arrive within two days to take on people from the "Atlantic". Although this was a welcome prospect, we observed the warlike activities all around and would rather have gone at once. Barbed wire emplacements, bunkers and trenches were springing up and it looked as if the storm would break at any moment. Such news as got through was announced over a megaphone, but there was little to report. Storfer and Goldner had gone ashore and they alone knew what was really going on. They stayed at a hotel and had contacts with the Romanians who seemed to regard them as V.I.P.'s. Some wild rumours accused Storfer of having been a Nazi spy under Schuschnigg, in return for which he had received permission after the "Anschluss" to make money out of organising illegal refugee transports. This just shows what fantasies some people were capable of. The megaphone announced that we would land in Palestine within six to ten days.

One of the Danzigers committed suicide. The last few days had been more than he could take. Other suicide attempts followed. Then Storfer appeared at long last, surrounded by a Haganah guard. They tried to protect him from the excited mob. He made some wild statements and threatened to remove the Schönbrunners who had become rather unpopular, but that was, of course, totally unacceptable. When it came to the crunch we were fellow Jews, after all, and literally in the same boat. At length an official Romanian commission arrived whom Storfer wanted to confirm that the vessel was seaworthy. The Romanians would do anything for money and duly obliged. Further provisions arrived. These mainly consisted of maggoty pulses and there was food, of a sort, for the next two days. The transport leaders had asked for three weeks' supplies, but Storfer promised that food and fuel would be available at Istanbul and that a fourth ship, the "Rosita" would arrive very shortly bringing provisions from Greece and a captain and crew. It was agreed that some engineers, toolmakers and other tradesmen from amongst ourselves could bring the crew up to full strength and that they would even be paid. In the event they did not receive a penny. It will never be known whether or not the captain had pocketed the money himself.

On 30th September a water main burst. The water ran down the staircase and flooded our sleeping quarters. The "Rosita" appeared the following day. It had been feared that she would be quite useless, but as she approached amid cheers it became obvious that, though smaller, she was in much better shape than the "Atlantic". However, the Romanians had already declared the "Atlantic" seaworthy and none of us were transferred to the "Rosita" which remained in Tulçea.

The crew came aboard and started to sell tins of sardines, bars of chocolates and sausages which should have gone into the stores. Captain Spiro, a fat little red-faced Greek, set up a canteen and put our provisions up for sale. (The provisions were said to have been donated by the Jewish community of Greece.) Spiro and his crew were a rare collection of crooks who constantly found ways of robbing us of what little we had left. Watches, lighters and fountain pens were traded for bits of food. A hawker came on board with sweets every day and he offered to supply whatever was ordered and paid for, but the captain soon put a stop to that to protect his monopoly.

Nine hundred lifebelts were delivered which were used as pillows at first. They had to be handed in again presently, but many were hidden away. When the ship was searched 300 of them were recovered and they were cut into two so that each passenger should have half a lifebelt in an emergency. The "Atlantic" lay at Tulçea for 23 days. Thinking of the "Pencho", we were beginning to wonder whether we would ever leave Romania. People were developing a collective claustrophobia and became irritable and aggressive. The crew inspired little confidence, yet some women began to consort with them for a hot meal. A number of them were later found to have contracted venereal diseases. There may have been prostitutes on board, but it was hardly surprising that desperation and hunger had driven others to this extremity. Theft also became a problem.

Many people would report sick. Doctors and nurses worked under impossible conditions. Their selfless service will always be remembered with gratitude. My cough grew worse and was aggravated by being unable to sit up in the bunk. I could get no sleep at all and was given some codeine, but the drug soon ran out. All manner of improvised mixtures followed, but, what with the prevailing dampness all around, these did not do much good. I stumbled up the stairs and looked for somewhere to rest awhile and get some fresh air. There was no room anywhere, even the lifeboats were being slept in and people squatted on the bridge.

Some tried to sleep standing, leaning on a pillar or on another person. The town lay way in the distance on the other side of the wide estuary. It was flooded by moonlight. Steeples and minarets stood out clearly. The water looked as black and as ominous as the future. If only we were leaving, overcrowded as we were, without any further delay and procrastination, away from the barges decorated with swastikas which were loading grain and oil for the Reich, away from the Iron Guard and their pogroms! Better to take a chance on mine-infested waters and on the hazards of heavy seas on an unseaworthy coffin ship than wait to die from starvation and disease in Tulçea.

The bottom bunk was occupied by the Silbersteins, a very nice young couple from Brno. They fetched my rations and this was a great help because I could not stand in line for any length of time and an hour's wait was by no means uncommon. The food was issued late in the afternoon and consisted of a kind of soup. I had already lost much weight. On the 6th of October two more people died, one of them a man of 70 who had fallen and injured his back.

When I managed to get on deck I would stand behind the funnel under a tarpaulin above the engine room which was spread out in hot weather. I discovered the spot quite by chance. I would sit down on a little folding stool that I had brought along from Bratislava. It served me well all through the voyage. Unfortunately the smoke drifting from the kitchen would make me gasp for breath.

On October 6th the boilers of the ship's engines were lit and smoke rose from the funnels. The luggage and the ballast chips from the "catacombs" were redistributed in an attempt to improve the balance because the ship had been listing one way or the other and water had run into the food stores. The sick bay was astern, well below the water line and in constant danger of being flooded. A whistle was blown ordering people to port or to starboard in an effort to compensate for the list; the "Atlantic" had no wireless equipment and was short of nautical instruments. Eventually one of our electricians improvised a system of bell relays which connected the bridge with the engine room. The crew were completely "at sea". In that sense, if in no other, they were well qualified for the job. People celebrated Rosh Hashanah shouting "Next year in Jerusalem!". They had gathered together in groups and prayed with a fervour never felt before.

On October 7th at 9 am. the sirens gave a forceful blast which was strangely out of character for the decrepit "Atlantic" whose English engine number plates dated back to 1870. The supply of coal had been difficult, but now there was enough for 10 days. We first moved upstream, intending to turn round at the next river bend, but the ship had hardly got going when she moved toward the bank and ran aground.

Communications between the bridge and the engine room had

broken down and the captain's commands had to be relayed by shouting from man to man. This went on for two hours. The ship had to reverse, but this was easier said than done. Another siren blast—this time a call for assistance. Motor launches appeared and one of them brought Storfer and Goldner. Eventually the ship got free. The start of our sea journey had not exactly been auspicious. We shuddered at the prospect that lay ahead. The "Atlantic" backed into the central navigation channel, but instead of staying there she made straight for the opposite bank and stopped only just in time to avoid running aground once again. The crowds who lined the bank and who watched with fascination retreated, lest they were run down on the bank by a mad invader from the river. In the event the ship scraped the bottom, but managed to return to the navigable channel where she dropped anchor. She had a pronounced starboard list and the passengers had to move to port to restore the balance. We were still waiting for the pilot who was to take us down the delta to Sulina. The "Atlantic" had been supposed to lead, but the steering gear had broken down. The "Pacific" and the "Milos" passed while we watched with apprehension. Three weeks earlier the "Pencho" had passed by without stopping, flying the Bulgarian flag. She had been marooned at Rustchuk for three months, but had finally made it, after all.

That day a woman died. Her children had been expecting her in Palestine. The bench between the hospital and the dispensary became an improvised mortuary. It was rarely unoccupied. The body was wrapped in blankets and an oil lamp stood there at night. People had to pass by on the way to "Panama".

The next morning the pilot turned up and the "Atlantic" was slowly towed down the river to Sulina where she arrived about five hours later. The name of the tug was "Ismael" and her skipper communicated with our captain by shouting in Romanian. The passage was tedious, though somewhat enlivened by the ship's propensity to run aground yet again, but the pilot knew his job well enough. We anchored at Sulina where the steering gear was to be repaired. We saw little of the town other than a few houses and taverns along the waterfront and a hotel with a dirty facade which looked even more disreputable than the shacks around it. Our Greek captain went ashore and returned with a group of officials. An hour later we pulled out to sea. The other arms of the delta were visible to the North and yellow streaks of brackish water reached far out.

The sea gradually turned green and then black as we went on, with the pilot still taking us in tow. A seaworthiness trial was about to commence. The "Atlantic" went round in a large circle. The steering was clearly defective and needed repair, but apart from some tools owned by the passengers, there was no tool kit on board. Storfer wanted the broken part to be patched up in Tulçea, but our people, afraid of a breakdown on the high seas, insisted that a repair job was impossible. The broken part had to be replaced. A new one had been obtained in Sulina overnight while the "Atlantic" had been moored offshore. The ship was rolling and many became seasick. Moans echoed through the "catacombs" and some who were staggering up to the deck arrived there too late. Fortunately paper bags had been issued the previous day.

The tug "Unica" appeared during the small hours of October 9th and the new part was successfully fitted. The "Milos" passed and the smoke from her funnel disappeared on the horizon. It was announced that the "Pencho" had got stuck in Turkish waters and that a Turkish ship was taking them to Palestine. The "Unica" stood by for over an hour, observing our progress and watching the captain's handling of the ship. Then she hooted farewell and her crew waved good luck and bon voyage. Our siren gave a mighty roar in reply. The body of the woman who had died two days earlier was lowered into the sea.

We had now been aboard the "Atlantic" for close on four weeks, but no communal spirit had as yet been established. There were quarrels and brawls. The Haganah blew their whistles and parted the combatants. This was not without danger since the Schönbrunners had knives. An engineering graduate from Prague broke an elderly man's nose and had to be restrained in a coal bunker for several days. He was let out eventually because his wife and baby needed him, but he was expelled from his Zionist group in disgrace.

The colour of the Black Sea really was black. The weather was fine and the waters were calm as the "Atlantic" bravely ploughed on. We were in luck, for this was the time of year when sudden gales were liable to blow up and make better ships than ours run for shelter in a hurry. The outline of the Bulgarian coast receded. Dolphins played in our crested wake. We were making good progress. The boilers were at maximum pressure and the furnaces were blazing away. The captain seemed to be in a great hurry, but for reasons different from ours. He wanted to use up fuel as fast as possible so as to have an excuse for calling at a Greek port, claiming that he would not be likely to get enough coal for the remainder of the journey in Istanbul. It was only later that we realised that he was wasting fuel so as to profiteer from the ensuing shortage.

It was early evening when we entered the Bosphorus where the promontories of Asia and Europe converge. Beyond this the sea opens out again into a gigantic lake. Elegant cafés and hotels lined the shore and crowds thronged floodlit terraces. The sound of dance music drifted over to us. I wondered how much longer these people would be able to enjoy themselves. I looked across without envy. How often do the very people who are happy and prosperous one moment become the most wretched of men presently!

We reached Istanbul in the evening. The city links two continents and the minarets of the mosques were brightly illuminated. The lights of the modern buildings and embankment boulevards were mirrored in the shimmering waters. A new world seemed to beckon. Sleek and sprightly ferries plied between Europe and Asia Minor. They would momentarily focus their light upon us while the passengers looked up in curious amazement.

We were nibbling some mouldy stuff which, according to Storfer, was suppose to be biscuits. They were hard as granite. The mould at first glance looked like icing sugar and had to be scraped off. More people became sick. The bread had run out and, apart from the daily issue of soup, there were only those wretched biscuits. The "Atlantic" became even more disgustingly filthy. Crowded and unable to pack together any more tightly we could neither wield a broom nor throw buckets of water over the deck.

We usually crawled into our bunks as the sun went down. There was no electric lighting and kerosene for the oil lamps was short, but that night we stayed up late. I rose early next morning and went on deck to see the sun rise over the imposing palaces of the sultans whose power had withered away. Their conquests had take them as far as Vienna. Two beautiful mosques stood close to the palace. The elegant minarets caught the first rays of the sun and reflected them from the golden pinnacles. The splendour of the Orient lay before us. Modern office building, banks, hotels and the main post office lined the opposite seafront. A snow white yacht was moored in front of the palace.

Most of us had not had a decent meal since leaving Bratislava, but the sight of this fabulous city made us forget our empty stomachs. We looked back with nostalgia and with a feeling of irrevocable loss, but without regret. We were glad to leave Europe behind and looked across towards Asia Minor with curiosity and with hope for there lay our future.

The Jewish community of Istanbul knew that we were coming and they had promised food and coal for the next morning, but the captain denied that there was any coal where he was supposed to pick it up. Turkish police came on board and warned us not to accept any packets from strangers for fear of a bomb plot. The Germans had occupied Romania and we had just got away in the nick of time.

The captain decided to move on that same evening although he knew about the food and the fuel that were due to arrive the next morning. He had taken on plenty of supplies for himself and his crew, but for us he had only bought 150 loaves of bread The rest of the journey should not have taken more than four or five days. With careful economy and proper planning there might even have been enough coal without any additional supplies, but it was the captain's intention to go island hopping in the Aegean and to get hold of part of any money that might be raised for us in each place.

That night we passed through the olive green waters of the Sea of Marmara and on October 11th we celebrated Yom Kippur. Many people were fasting, some because they were observant Jews, others because of necessity. In any case, there was no food cooked that day.

The scenery intruded upon the devotions of prayer. The light grey outline of the coast was far away. The crested waves were a delectable sight and the overcrowding became somehow more bearable as the engines plodded away, for we were nearing our destination. The shortage of food bothered us less than the shortage of coal. Provided only that there was enough coal we would manage on Storfer's mouldy biscuits.

We entered the Dardanelles at sunrise of October 12th and passed several towns and villages, as well as many military encampments. We noticed some numerals on rocky promontories and on gentle slopes. White stones commemorated the great battles of Gallipoli of the First World War. Much blood had been spilled here. The cemeteries bore more eloquent witness to man's folly than the victory inscriptions in white stone mosaic, or the famous obelisk of Kum-Kalek, which presently came into view. We looked at the ruins of the medieval fortifications and at the camouflaged emplacements whose gun muzzles one could just make out. No warship or merchantman was in sight. We arrived at Kebel Sultania just before noon. The Turkish police left after checking the transit visas once more, making sure that nobody had got off the ship. We sailed into the Aegean and passed one rocky uninhabited island after another while the last reserves of coal were being brought up from the bunkers. At half past eight in the evening we reached Lesbos and anchored in the port of Mytilene, but not before we had our first experience of a storm at sea. The "Atlantic" was tossed about and one can imagine the effect on the passengers. As for myself, I only felt an overpowering weakness as the pounding of the elements reverberated throughout the ship. I was plagued by spasms of coughing, but once we had reached port and saw the bright lights of the little town and its promenade all seemed well.

Next morning we had a good view of Mytilene, a pretty holiday resort which rises on gentle slopes and has many modern hotels and villas. There were cottages with brightly coloured umbrellas in the gardens and on the balconies. It was a charming place and it would have been nice to rest there for a while. Sailors strolled around in white uniforms and a military band played as it marched along the promenade and up a sloping side street. Children could be seen running to the seafront and small fishing craft bobbed about in the harbour. Barrels of wine were rolled into taverns and all seemed neat and peaceful. We remained at Mytilene until the late afternoon of October 13th. Another woman died.

Food and coal were unobtainable. The captain was either unable or unwilling to pay and there was no Jewish community to come to our aid. Next morning we reached Karlovarti on Samos, an island with well tended vineyards. Steep rocks made access difficult. We noted the now familiar wine casks, taverns, shops and fishing smacks and I recalled Schiller's "Ring of Polykrates". Again we were unable to obtain either food or fuel. The captain was just wasting time. We were off again at mid morning. A crowd of people stood along the quay and a priest was saying a blessing over the "Atlantic". It was nice to know that some people had compassion and wished us well.

Another big storm had gathered and again the "Atlantic" was tossed about. The seas, the heavens and even the stars seemed to be in turmoil. The "catacombs" now had to accommodate those who normally stayed on deck as well, and one can imagine the scene while gigantic waves pounded the hull. Many who had resigned themselves to being shipwrecked were praying for a merciful release. In mid afternoon the engines stopped and we heard the rattle of the anchor chain. We had arrived at the little town of Nyos, which lies in a picturesque bay in the shelter of massive mountains. A small snow white chapel stood on the tip of a rocky promontory. It had a steeple with a round top and looked as if it had been sculpted from a sugar loaf by a clever confectioner. Standing in the bright sunshine against the background of a deep blue sky it looked particularly charming. We left at 9 p.m. Another storm arose and tossed us about all through the night, but we were getting accustomed to this and were no longer much bothered by sea sickness. Sleep, of course, was out of the question, the more so as we were often ordered to port or to starboard in order to correct the imbalance caused by the list of the ship. The kitchens were out of action because the "soup" from the pots had doused the fires. According to the captain we were now passing the Italian-held islands of the Dodecanese. He was scared out of his wits. The captain, his first officer Dacosta and all the crew had made sure of their lifebelts and the Panamanian flag was brightly illuminated during darkness.

We arrived at Heraklion (Crete) on October 16th and anchored in the outer harbour. New harbour facilities were being constructed and concrete mixers were churning away. The town is largely situated on a plateau and out of sight. We were only able to see the part around the harbour. The inner harbour was a good distance away, but it was as busy as a beehive. The health authorities had heard rumours of a dysentery epidemic on the "Atlantic" and would not allow her anywhere near the jetty; but there were lots of rowing boats with curious sightseers. Some Greeks tried to do business and offered to buy cigarette lighters and fountain pens from us. A variety of articles began to change hands, but the captain quickly clamped down on the trade.

There was a refugee committee in Heraklion headed by a Mr. Sevilla. He represented the "Joint" and it was entirely due to him that we were able to continue our journey. A cable to Storfer brought the answer that he (Storfer) could do no more for us. Mr. Sevilla appealed to the Greek Jewish community and raised enough money to buy some low-grade coal and a minimum of provisions. It took 22 days for the coal to arrive from Piraeus. Another woman died; her coffin was draped in blankets and roped to the ship's side. She was later buried in the local cemetery.

Some bread arrived the next day and drinking water was brought up by tanker. It was pumped up with hose-pipes, a notable technological advance on the bucket method. The fresh water was mainly reserved for cooking. The following night there was torrential rain and we had to bale out with buckets, an activity which lasted well into the next day, by which time the skies had cleared. All the stuff on deck had got soaked. I felt very weak and had great difficulty getting up there.

A boat brought fresh vegetables, wine, eggs and butter for the sick and the doctor secured some additional food for me. The wine had been watered down, but the crooks had not even bothered to use fresh water for the purpose. Some people were seen to clutch bottles which they had bought from some who had robbed the sick and infirm.

On October 21st it was announced that we would have to make for Piraeus for fuel, because there was not enough coal on Crete, but the coal from Piraeus arrived two days later and was loaded into the bunkers. All the able-bodied men were helping. The ballast was moved again and the Panamanian colours were prominently painted on both sides of the funnels, so that passing aircraft could readily identify the "Atlantic" as a neutral ship. We were supposed to make a straight run for Haifa now, although the official manifest stated: "Destination Shanghai, with a scheduled call at Port Said". We heard that the "Pencho" had got stranded and had sunk, but most of the passengers were reportedly safe and they had been interned by the Italians on Rhodes, though a number of injured had been left on the wreckage. The number of victims was not disclosed. Meanwhile one of the children on the "Atlantic" died.

At 10.30 that evening the anchor was raised and we left harbour. The waves pounded the hull, but we were glad to be on our way. The dismay was all the greater when the engines stopped and we realised that we were back in Heraklion. Our leaders questioned the captain. He declared that the coal was useless. There wasn't much left anyway. We suspected that coal had been surreptitiously dumped during the one-and-a-half hours' cruise out of Heraklion so as to sabotage our journey. The captain had been paid his wages in advance when the "Atlantic" left Tulçea and the only money still due to him was a premium on reaching Haifa.

It did not escape our attention that the crew were wearing lifebelts during the Heraklion episode. The Haganah kept the lifeboats under constant observation from then on, lest the crew were planning to jump ship and abandon us, which they were quite capable of doing. They were obviously fed up and scared stiff of floating mines and of Italian aircraft. Moreover, they had little confidence in the "Atlantic" or her skipper. The ship had neither wireless nor proper navigational instruments, her boiler was full of scale and the furnaces were choked with clinker. But they were well paid for the risks, while for us the "Atlantic" was the only hope.

On October 25th a large quantity of provisions suddenly arrived. We had been down to a cup of tea and a bowl of "soup" a day. The unexpected influx of food offered a fine opportunity for thievery. Accusations were bandied about and fights followed, but the actual mention of the theft of rations (which, of course, it was all about) was taboo. The Haganah had double rations and special issues and they certainly deserved these. Voluntary workers could also earn some extra food, so we suddenly had 70 stokers working in shifts, with seven on duty at any one time. But some received little more than before and there was an early end to the unexpected bonanza.

The skipper went ashore every night, despite the warnings and the remonstrances of the harbour master. Tension between the captain and the passengers increased. A scandal was discovered which involved the first officer and the wife of a Danziger. It seemed that we were fated to be stuck in Greece. There was food enough for eight days, but we could not go on without an adequate supply of fuel. The dumped coal may well have been of poor quality, but it was still coal of sorts and a judicious mix with decent stuff would have made the resumption of the journey a reasonable proposition.

Life was dominated by queues—queues for tea, for water, for bread, for soup, for the doctor, for the dispensary, for "Panama". One had to eat standing while others stood on one's toes. It was dark and one could not be sure what one was eating, which was perhaps just as well. Only those who slept on deck were allowed to take their meals there. This was fair, because they had the worst of the weather. Those who slept in the "catacombs" had to put up with the stench, the smoke and the filth at mealtimes, but they also fetched buckets of seawater down to do the laundry. I had become indifferent to being scalded by hot tea and to kicks and elbow jabs and was willing to put up with anything, so long as there still remained some hope of seeing my wife and my sons again at the end of it all.

We woke up on October 26th and saw to our great surprise that the "Milos" had entered the harbour. She had come from Piraeus with coal and provisions during the night. Her captain had jumped ship and one of the engineers among the refugees was the new master. Nobody knew what had happened to the "Pacific". The "Milos" left the same morning. A man died. A child was born.

Some officials came to inspect the boilers and promised to find coal for us. Two days later Italy invaded Greece. The government commandeered all fuel stocks and it became extremely doubtful whether we would ever be able to get any coal now. Moreover, there were only four days' provisions left. Further food supplies required an export licence and that, apparently, could only be obtained from Athens. All the usual harbour traffic ceased. A British aircraft flew over the town and a number of our young men thought of volunteering for the Greek army. On November 5th we received 50 tons of coal and more was promised for the following day.

Italian aircraft now posed an additional threat. The Italians had already bombed several ports. The papers said that Heraklion had been raided, though there had been no damage. We watched the anti-aircraft batteries blazing away at night and saw the sky light up intermittently far out at sea. A naval battle seemed to be in progress and the "Atlantic" rehearsed "air raid precautions". Under no circumstances was the ship to get anywhere near the pier, lest anybody get ashore. The captain and one of his crew made for the lifeboat at the first sound of the siren, but the Haganah turned them back. On the next occasion they made a second and more successful try and actually got ashore. They had hoped to disappear in town, but the pair of them were brought back under an army escort.

I was getting very weak. The Silbersteins from Brno and dear old Nettl from Reichenberg took turns fetching my rations. The four of us shared the few tins of emergency food from Bratislava to which we had held on till now. Young Mrs. Silberstein would light the oil stove and each of us had a mouthful. We remembered the days when hunger had not yet been a constant travelling companion. The reserves were soon exhausted.

The skipper had a fair amount of experience of extracting the last penny from the passengers because he had been on similar journeys before. Traders in small boats brought grapes and other fruit alongside and the captain made a handsome middleman's profit. As in Istanbul, he prevented gifts from reaching us. He even refused to allow the supplies on board that had already been paid for by the local Jewish community. He enforced his trade monopoly and dictated the prices, knowing that we could only pay or starve. His example was imitated by the crew and even corrupted some of our own fellow passengers. The girl friend of a cook in the Praguers kitchen once gave me an extra pint of tea in exchange for a whole tin of sardines.

The last of the coal was loaded on November 5th. The authorities demanded that we depart without further delay. British and Greek aircraft were frequently overhead. The captain wanted to make for Athens, allegedly "to obtain information and directives", but he was not allowed on the mail steamer. Another woman died on November 7th; she was the wife of a man who had been buried on Crete. Next day officials arrived; they insisted that we leave at once and wished us luck. Safety belts were issued and people were formed into groups which were assigned assembly points, but it was a mystery how we were to get out of the "catacombs" in an emergency. Fortunately, the matter was never put to the test.

Rubbish was dropped down the shaft, some carelessly, some for a "joke", but we paid little attention; we were more concerned with the threat of torpedoes from enemy warships. The tension of the past weeks, the squabbles requiring constant intervention by the Haganah, the sickness and the hunger had made us apathetic. Some people would have welcomed anything if only it would have meant the end of the ceaseless noise, the jostling, the stench and the dirt.

We finally left Heraklion at 8.30. The pounding of the waves and the stamping of the engines were sweet music now. But at 7 in the evening the anchor chains rattled and there was a lot of shouting from the deck. The captain had got the wind up again and was funking the journey. He had circled the island and the "Atlantic" was now in the bay of St. Nikolo. This was one of the loveliest spots of our Aegean cruise, but we were not in a sightseeing mood. Our men had tried to stop the lowering of the anchor, but they were too late. Under the leadership of young Dr. Horetzky from Prague the captain was separated from the crew. He was forced into his cabin and the harbour master was informed. He phoned Heraklion and gave us his full support. Had it not been for Dr. Horetzky's energetic action we would never have left the idyllic bay, except for eventual deportation by the Germans. We continued to plod along. The engine room, the coal bunkers and the stores were now guarded by our own men. All the orders from the captain were carefully checked. He was under constant surveillance by two of our strongest lads and they never left him for a moment.

The coal was of very poor quality. The Greeks had swindled us with the coal as others had swindled us with mouldy biscuits and maggoty beans. The crew were not allowed anywhere near the boiler room or the engines. All the work was done by our own men, of whom some had useful skills, but at about 6.30 the engines stopped. The coal did not burn sufficiently well to raise enough steam. The islands of the Dodecanese were not far away, but gentle currents caused the "Atlantic" to drift south and they gradually disappeared from sight. Meanwhile our men had doused the fire in the furnaces, removed the clinker and raised a fresh fire. On November 9th this routine was repeated twice more. Our progress was painfully slow. The stokers tried to raise the calorific value of the coal dust by adding wood, starting with boxes and loose planks.

On the 11th of November the Greek crew sent a deputation with the request that they be allowed to resume duties. They had been kept away from all navigational work but, bearing in mind that the ship's safety was in their interest as much as in ours, this was agreed to. The captain also sued for peace and his assurances were accepted because his assessment of the quality of the coal had been confirmed, even though his cowardice, the sabotage, the treachery and the profiteering deserved the severest punishment. But we were on the high seas again and the greedy blighter's expectation of the outstanding bonus on arrival could perhaps be relied upon to serve as an incentive.

The previous night we had heard naval guns in the distance for several hours and it seemed that the dull thuds and the sporadic flickers of light had been coming from a northwesterly direction. We began to burn the superstructure and the furniture. Axes were wielded on planks and railings. Nothing was spared. Life itself depended on firing away with this last resource of fuel. The dining room panelling, the old peoples' dormitories, all these went. Floorboards, doors, cabin walls and partitions were ripped out. The bow of the ship was entirely stripped of all timber. Everybody except the children stayed where they were. Human chains conveyed every scrap of wood to the furnaces. The captain, scared by the night's naval engagement, wanted to return to Crete. He was ignored and eventually abandoned his voluble protests.

5. Cyprus and Haifa Harbour

On 11th two warships appeared on the horizon. The "Atlantic" stopped, knowing that she was a sitting duck. There was much excitement and people wondered whether the ships were British or Italian. We flashed light signals and asked for assistance, saying that there was only one day's supply of food and hardly any drinking water left and that we were unable to make port under our own steam. The warships came closer and looked us all over. They were British and signalled that they were unable to do anything for us, but that they would summon help. Meanwhile the sun had set. The ships slipped away as quickly and as gracefully as they had appeared and were soon swallowed up in the gathering darkness. All the available timbers had to go into the furnaces now, the floorboards, encrusted with dirt as they were, the mast, the hoists, the bunks, the remaining partitions. The work of cannibalisation continued at first light and was pursued with ruthless determination. It was the only means of raising steam. Fortunately the weather remained fine and the sea was calm. We could not possibly have withstood another onslaught of the elements. The Haganah had obtained definite proof that coal had been dumped overboard by the crew in an attempt to sabotage our departure from Greece. That day we had to make three stops in order to decoke the furnaces. Each time it took several hours to raise steam again. On November 13th some men went on strike for improved rations although there was practically no food left. But the stokers were on the point of collapse through sheer physical exhaustion and it was only thanks to their heroic labour that we survived to tell the tale.

The following night the "Atlantic" limped along at a snail's pace and continuously sent out SOS signals in Morse code. Land was sighted at first light. The captain insisted that it was an Italian island and begged us to back off. Then he changed his mind and claimed that it was the coast of Anatolia. A final all-out effort was made. Anything combustible went into the furnaces and the "Atlantic" became just one large shapeless hulk. Everybody was utterly exhausted. I had received permission to sit on the bridge ever since we left Heraklion.

This was a great boon since I could not stand the "catacombs" any longer, what with the stench of excrement and sea sickness, not to mention the smoke from the galleys and the lack of breathable air. I had been gasping for breath and was unable to stretch my legs. I had become apathetic and the prospect of shipwreck began to offer a merciful release.

We were within sight of land when the engines finally stopped. Anything that looked remotely like a combustible item had been used up. The captain ordered that the Turkish flag be hoisted, but it did not stay up long. A motor launch approached, flying the Union Jack. We in turn ran up the British flag amid rejoicing. The "Atlantic" was off Cyprus and close to Limassol. A tug took her in tow and she reached harbour by 7 p.m. A miracle! We had made it! And without expert seamanship or modern navigational equipment! Cyprus, indeed, with nothing left apart from a few mouldy biscuits and just enough water to brew a drop of tea in the morning!

November 14th. An inspection commission arrived on board. The "Atlantic" (or what was left of her) had been tidied up as much as possible, but she still looked an awful mess. We were told that we could have coal, provided we paid for it. The Schönbrunners and the Danzigers still had some foreign exchange left, even though they had squandered a lot on silly luxuries on the way down the Danube. Watches and jewellery were acceptable currency. Gentle persuasion had to be used on some who could not bear to part, which was odd, considering what the very same people would have given to save their lives just hours before. The Haganah searched the luggage of those who refused to contribute. The dispensary handed in a few items from the medical stores which might raise some cash. There were incredible scenes at the "canteen". The captain and Dacosta had brought food on board. They now offered it at fantastic prices. Some people were keen to buy so as to avoid having to contribute to the collection. There was an upright piano which had somehow been overlooked in the quest for firewood. It, too, was exchanged for coal. All the brass fittings were stripped and sold off. There was plenty of everything on the island, provided one could pay for it, but nobody seemed to care. They did not realise that the refugees were practically destitute and that most of us had not been allowed to take any money with them, apart from those few worthless German marks. Very few had much in the way of jewellery other than their wedding rings.

There were arguments among individuals and among groups about how much they were to contribute. The wedding ring was my only article of any value. It was hard to part with it, but it had become the price of survival and so represented the only hope of an eventual family reunion. It symbolised the future as much as the past. A few years ago it had been too small; now I had to take care lest it drop off my finger. I remembered the synagogue wedding in the Schmalzhofgasse, the reception at the Hotel de France and our first home in the Blechturmgasse. Parting with the ring now was an act of faith and a symbol of hope. Silently begging my wife's forgiveness I handed it in. A girl of 17 died.

Sightseers and traders came alongside. The Haganah confiscated what foreign exchange they could find. They bought a few oranges and gave them to the children. By the 16th November some £500 had been raised, enough for all the food and fuel needed to take us to Haifa. The first consignment of coal arrived and the remainder was promised during the next few days. Provisions were taken on, but no cooking was possible until the evening and no food was available all day. The cooks were exhausted. They were not able to do any work until they had eaten themselves.

On November 17th we made the headlines in the Cypriot press. The papers wrote about our escape from the Nazis and how we managed to slip through the Italian minefields. They wrote about the bombing, the hunger and the thirst, the disease and the death roll, how we had had to cannibalise the ship and burn two tons of timber each day, but nothing was said about coal. Our escape had been narrow indeed. We had been very lucky in that a northerly wind had pushed us towards Cyprus rather than towards the Dodecanese or back to Crete. We were still at Limassol on November 19th. It was rumoured that we might be interned on the island. Four very sick people were taken to the hospital in town.

The transport leaders were asked where we were making for. They replied, diplomatically, that we would very much like to go to Palestine since many of us had relatives there, but that our papers had been made out for Port Said. The officials smiled. A report of the conversation was given over the megaphone. The papers published an appeal and we received gifts of luscious oranges and grapefruit, new potatoes, butter, raisins and syrup. In order to prevent profiteering, all the gifts were distributed as soon as they arrived and everybody had a reasonable supply which could be used as one wished. More coal was delivered and morale soared. But unfortunately yet another woman died.

Next day the last of the coal was taken on. We were going to Haifa! Yet more food arrived and another cleaning-up operation was embarked upon. I could not imagine why such a lot of food was brought on board, considering that Haifa was just 18 hours' journey ahead. Would we be kept on board ship for some time, perhaps in quarantine, before being allowed to disembark?

Some of the food that arrived was quite fabulous and included items that we had long forgotten about—eggs, white flour, corned beef, sardines, even coffee and cocoa! We had two good meals a day and plenty of oranges and grapefruit. The Silbersteins and Nettl fetched my rations. That evening there was a fireworks party on board; the Greeks had won a great victory over the Italians near the Albanian town of Koritza and the crew were ecstatic with jubilation. There were Roman candles and Catherine wheels and the captain even wanted to send up some rockets in celebration, but the harbour police soon put a stop to that because of the blackout.

During the night a British officer arrived with a platoon of soldiers. We had to squeeze together even more tightly to make room for them. For the first time during our journey the bridge was hosed down and at 5 a.m. we were off on what we fondly imagined was to be the last lap of our odyssey. A feeling of euphoria took hold of me. We were to get off the "Atlantic" at last! We were going to land in Haifa and we even had a guard of honour! No further tricks from the Greek captain—the British were in command. We proceeded very slowly. A loaded freighter was following behind. Wireless equipment and anti-aircraft guns were installed We had been at sea for some hours and could still see the peaks of Cyprus when the mountains of Lebanon appeared on the Eastern horizon. There were happy faces everywhere, people were singing, accompanied by harmonicas and violins and there would have been dancing too had space permitted. The horrors of the past had begun to recede.

The outline of the Carmel appeared, bathed in the glorious light of the rising sun. People were shouting with joy. Haifa itself came into view, a large and modern city with new apartment blocks and smart villas ascending the slopes. We anchored just outside the harbour and beheld a great industrial complex with busy traffic. The "Pacific" and the "Milos" were there as well, but no smoke belched out of their chimneys and they were evidently deserted. I wondered whether my

C o p y

All communications to be addressed to the Department and not to
individuals.

GERMAN JEWISH AID COMMITTEE
Immigration Department
Woburn House, Upper Woburn Place

Ref.No. BA/23743   London W.C.1

Karl Lenk Esq.,
Schottenfeldgasse 53,
Vienna VII/62,
Germany   22 AUG 1939

Dear Sir /Madam,

    We have pleasure in advising you that we have to-day heard
from the Home Office to the effect that a communication regarding
the granting of your visa has been sent to the British Passport
Control Officer in Vienna who will, as soon as possible, invite you
to call.
    Kindly note that no useful purpose will be served by applying
to the British Passport Officer before such communication is
received.
    We would also point out that immediatly on arrival in Great
Britain, you should report either in person or by letter to the
REGISTRATION DEPT. at BLOOMSBURY HOUSE, BLOOMSBURY STREET,
London, W.C.,1.

            Yours faithfully,
            German Jewish Aid Committee

            Signature illegible   Immigration Department

Copy of envelope:
    Stamp London W.C.1 10 15 pm 22 August 1939
            Road Users Take POST   e
            Avoid   STAMP s

    Karl Lenk Esq.,
        Schottenfeldgasse 53,
            Vienna VII/62, Germany   en appointment

2152

    C o p y   c e r t i f i e d   c o r r e c t

    Beau Bassin, Mauritius   Area Commandant
    March   7 th   1943   Detainment Camp

Plate II: Copy of a letter from the Jewish Aid Committee to
Karl Lenk advising him that he had been granted
a visa to enter Great Britain

i

Plate III: Woodcut by Perez B. Mayer

Plate IV: Woodcut by Perez B. Mayer

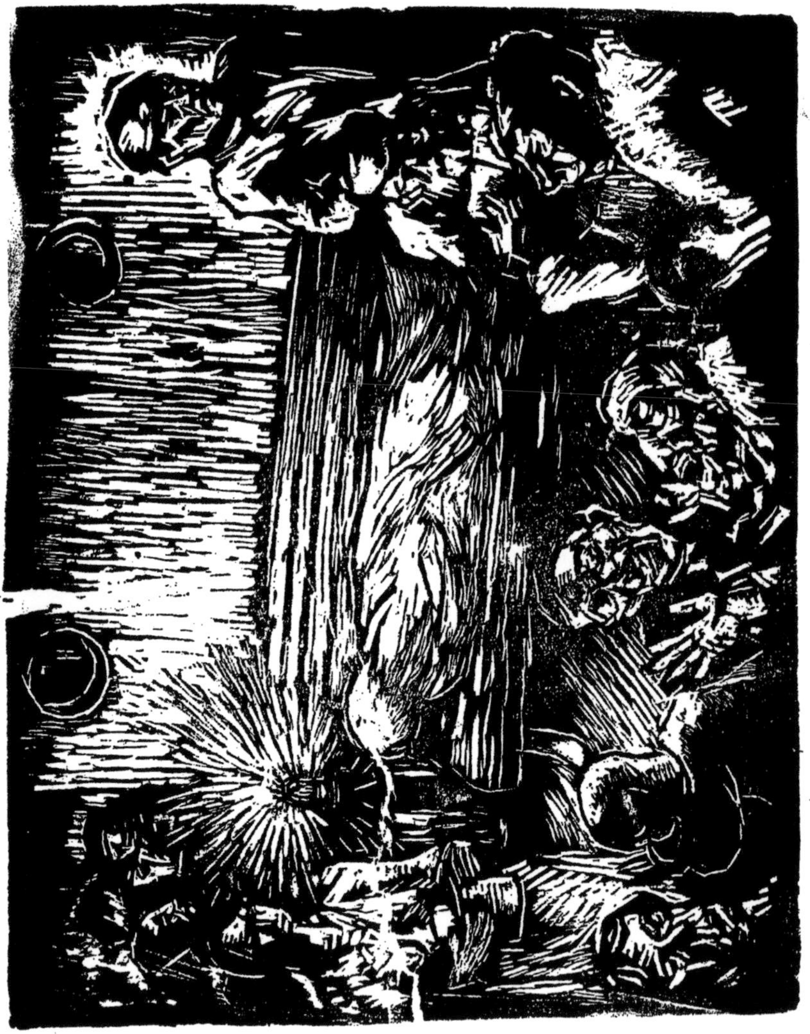

Plate V:
Woodcut by
Perez B. Mayer

Plate VI: Greek fruit seller
pen and ink drawing by F. Händel

Plate VII: Original woodcut (British Officer)
by F. Händel, 1943

Orig. Woodcut   F. Haendel 43

Plate VIII: Original woodcut (Palestine Police)
by F. Händel, 1943

Plate IXa: H.M. Prison, Beau Bassin

Plate IXB: H.M. Prison, Beau Bassin

Plate X: H.M. Prison, Beau Bassin
Woodcut by Perez B. Mayer

Plate XI: H.M. Prison, Beau Bassin. Woodcut by Perez B. Mayer

x

Plate XIIa:
Group of inmates at H.M. Prison, Beau Bassin

Plate XII: H.M. Prison, Beau Bassin

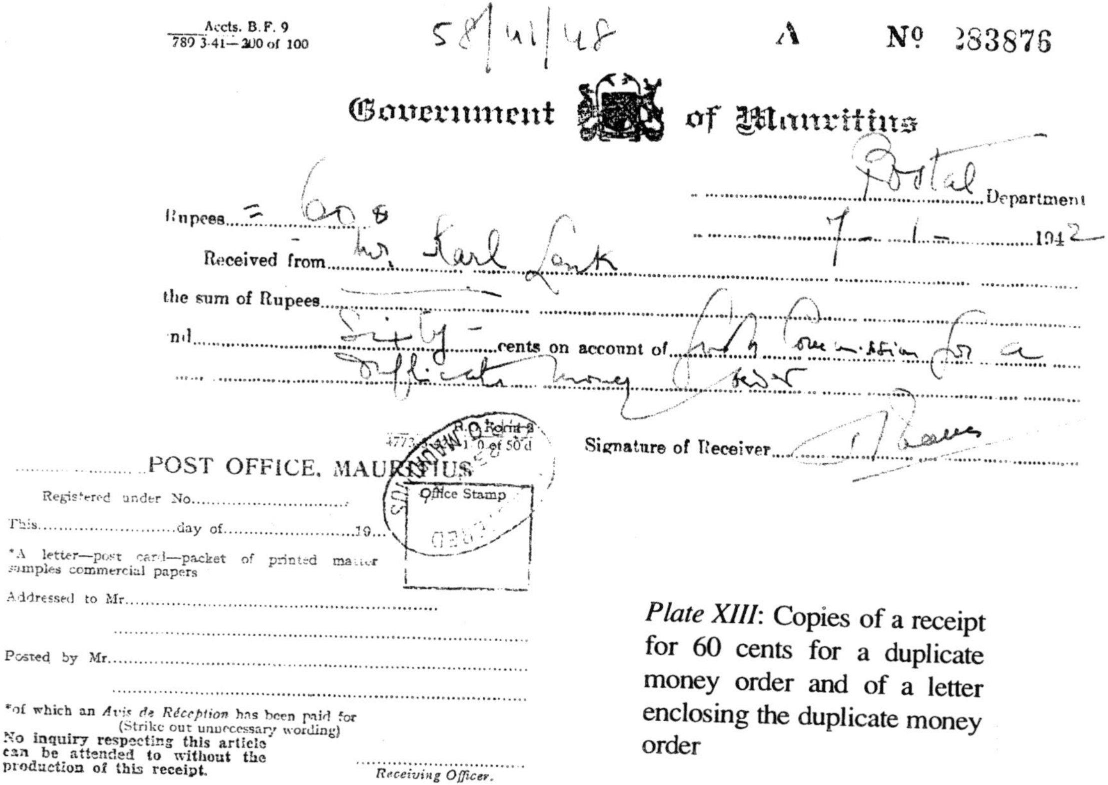

Accts. B.F. 9.
$\frac{780}{780}$ 3-41—200 of 100

A   No. 233876

Government of Mauritius

.... Department

.... 194 2

Rupees..

Received from...

the sum of Rupees...

nl................................. rents on account of..................

....

Signature of Receiver...

POST OFFICE, MAURITIUS.

Office Stamp

Registered under No..

This.............................day of...................19.......

*A letter—post card—packet of printed matter—
samples commercial papers

Addressed to Mr..

Posted by Mr..

*of which an *Avis de Réception* has been paid for
(Strike out unnecessary wording)
No inquiry respecting this article
can be attended to without the
production of this receipt.

.... *Receiving Officer.*

Plate XIII: Copies of a receipt
for 60 cents for a duplicate
money order and of a letter
enclosing the duplicate money
order

POST OFFICE OF PALESTINE.

P.T. 205

CUSTOMS DECLARATION.
(*DÉCLARATION EN DOUANE*)

PLACE OF POSTING.
(*LIEU DE DÉPART*)

PLACE OF DESTINATION.
(*LIEU DE DESTINATION.*)

Name and Address of Addressee — Mr. Kurt Lenk Munich via P.O.B. 1000

(*cf. (v. 1307)*)

39190—100000—72,12,35.—S.O.P.

Parcels (Colis postaux)		Contents (Désignation du contenu) To be described, in both French and English. (See note below)	Country of Origin *pays d'origine*	value of Contents (*valeur*)		Weight (*Poids*)	
Number (*Nombre*)	Description including special marks & numbers of the sender (*Espèce et marques et numéros spéciaux de l'expéditeur*)			L.P.	Mils	Gross (*brut*) K Gr.	Net (*net*) K Gr.
1	Linen used 2,10-13	personal effects	Palestine Germany	0	1	3 570 3	3 570

Stamp of Office of Posting (*Timbre du bureau de départ*)

OBSERVATIONS

N. B. — The nature and value of the contents should be accurately stated and, as far as possible, in accordance with the classification of the customs tariff of the country destination. The name of the country of origin, *i.e.*, the name of the country where the goods were produced or manufactured, should be given in all cases, whether it is Palestine or not, and the certificate overleaf should be signed.

P.I.O.

Plate XIV: Copies of a receipt for posted letter and of a Customs Declaration by Karl Lenk

xiii

Mauritius

BLOCK B
WARD 5
ZELLE 38
DET.- N! 1807
JUNI 1941

Plate XV: Drawing of Cell 38, H.M. Prison, Beau Bassin

Plate XVI: Drawing of Cell 38, H.M. Prison, Beau Bassin

Plate XVII: Grave of Karl Lenk, Mauritius, c. 1944

Plate XVIII: Jewish cemetery, Mauritius, 1980s

Plate XIX: Portrait of Karl Lenk and pictures of Mauritius detainees, Jewish Museum, Berlin

Plate XX: Dr. A. Zwergbaum (standing) with Mme. Geneviève
Pitot, Israel 1992

Plate XXI: A Nazi presence on British soil—troops march through the streets of Guernsey

Plate XXII: Nazi officers deploying slave labour

brother and my sister-in-law were living in one of the houses on the mountain slopes. Were they perhaps looking down on the "Atlantic" this very moment? Would they be able to pick me out with their field glasses? Tears of joy overwhelmed me. All would surely be well now.

Two large ferryboats arrived. Disembarkation started in the afternoon, women and children first. There were a lot of police around. Customs officials examined everything minutely and progress was exceedingly slow. The luggage was taken off separately. Documents, books, newspapers, letters and other hand-written material had to be handed in. Some of our escort from Cyprus accepted letters for posting to relatives. I handed in one addressed to my brother, but I had no money for a stamp and I do not know whether it ever reached him. I had been posting letters without stamps before, in Tulçea, in Istanbul and on the Greek islands, hoping that they might arrive somehow, but as far as I know none ever did.

All manner of disturbing rumours went around. There was a large grey ship in the distance, the "Patria", a 12,000 ton passenger liner with several decks. A tug was standing by and smoke rose from her three funnels. There were supposed to be people from the "Pacific" and from the "Milos" on board. They were to be deported. Where to? Surely, this was nonsense. Could it be that the "Patria" was merely a place of quarantine? Had she not been at anchor there for all of three weeks already? The rumours about our impending deportation persisted and Mauritius was mentioned. A map was brought along and there it was—an island in the Indian ocean east of Madagascar. This was surely absurd. The British could not be so callous as to deport us after all that we had been through, not to mention that such a journey would again expose us to the danger of passing within striking distance of Italian bases! No. It had to be a quarantine ship and we would be free soon. We watched uneasily as the first ferry-load left for the grey liner. After a night filled with nervous speculation a second boat-load was taken off in the morning followed by a third carrying mainly families with young children.

I was down in the "catacombs" at the time, but presently there was a tremendous commotion up above and everyone was frantically trying to get on deck. People stared towards the big grey ship—she had gone! There was frenzied activity in the harbour and motor launches were scuttling to and fro. Smoke hung over the spot where the ship had been only moments before. Something terrible had happened. How could a vessel of that size, with 2,000 people on board, have vanished so quickly?

The ferry that had just left the "Atlantic" returned. Its occupants had seen it all at close quarters. A sheet of flame had suddenly shot out from the side of the "Patria" and she had capsized almost at once. People had been flung into the water and were shouting for help. The ferry had picked up two of them. Months later it transpired that 205 people had lost their lives. Surely, after all this, they would let us stay and there would be no further talk of deportation? We wondered what had caused the tragedy. Arab terrorists? Nazi agents? I remembered the warning not to accept any parcels from strangers.

Next morning, November 27th, the "Atlantic" was slowly taken into the harbour. We saw the camouflaged oil tanks at close range. Women and children disembarked first and were taken to Atlit camp by bus. The survivors from the "Patria" had already arrived. There had been little rain during our journey, but now that the rainy season had started the heavens opened. The dirt and filth of the "Atlantic" was kneaded into a quagmire and it became so slippery that movement on board came to a virtual standstill.

Mrs Lenk with sons Rudi and Robert,
and with daughter-in-law Henny, London 1940

6. Akko and Atlit

November 28th. I was among a group which mainly consisted of bachelors and younger married men and it was our turn to disembark next. Broken suitcases were strewn around. After a great deal of jostling we reached the gangway to the jetty where coaches were waiting. The young man next to me had been unable to get hold of his suitcase in time and was roughly handled by a policeman who made him leave the ship without it. He very kindly helped me with my suitcase which friends from the "catacombs" had been carrying until then.

How marvellous to stand on dry land once again, to breathe fresh air and not to be sandwiched between bodies! The harbour was new and the customs hall, bustling with activity, was spotlessly clean. We were closely searched. All papers were impounded and receipts were issued. We were loaded into buses and Jewish drivers were taking us to disinfection stations. Our clothes were treated separately. Some people's heads were crawling with lice. All of us had our hair doused with a pungent liquid. We had a hot shower and our own doctors looked us over. It was only many months later that I learned how worried they had been about my emaciated state and how delighted they were that I had pulled through. I had been in such a poor condition that the doctors were not prepared to risk giving me typhoid and smallpox injections at the time. Dr. Kummermann thought that with my cough I would surely soon be released anyway.

Back on the buses, we were driven over well surfaced suburban roads. New buildings were rising everywhere. The street signs were in English, Hebrew and Arabic. We passed modest sized houses surrounded by colourful flowering shrubs. Heavily laden asses trudged along the pavements led by Arab boys. A wrecked house here and there bore silent witness to the prevailing state of civil unrest. Buses full of children passed by. A large Jewish school was being built. We saw the modern buildings of a rural kibbutz set in obviously lovingly tended fields which contrasted with the barren land further away, where the monotony of the landscape was further enhanced by the scrub and the occasional corrugated iron roofed shack. We passed through ancient Akko, whose narrow streets were surrounded by a medieval wall. The town stands on a tongue of land which is dominated by the green and golden roof of the mosque and by the minarets which gleamed in the sunshine. The bus skirted the town and we were relieved not to be taken to its infamous prison. Eventually the bus took a left turn and a barrack camp came into view, surrounded by a barbed wire fence.

We were taken to the "Office for Refugees", which seemed reassuring, inasmuch as there was another office which dealt with political prisoners. We were told that we would have to do our own cleaning, cooking and baking. Police supervised the issue of rations and the preparation of the food. The wooden barracks had corrugated iron roofs and accommodated thirty men each. People arranged themselves in the "traditional" manner—Schönbrunners, Danzigers, Viennese and Praguers. Everybody was given three new army blankets. We slept on the floor for the first two nights until wooden bedsteads and new mattresses arrived. The camp was situated on the seashore. A barbed wire fence ran 100 yards from the water but we only had access to the sandy beach. The commandant promised that we would be allowed to use a strip of the bathing beach. There were hot showers, proper sanitary facilities and plenty of space for exercise. It was quiet and peaceful and I could almost pretend to myself to be in a rest home as I sat on the hot sands of the beach. We had two roll calls per day and a curfew was in force between 7 in the evening and 7 in the morning. The suitcases had stayed behind in Haifa for disinfection and were not expected for a few days. We were promised "an easy time" if we "behaved ourselves" (whatever that meant), but we were also warned of severe punishment (this puzzled us!) if we didn't.

Any contact with the "politicals" was strictly forbidden. These were mostly Jewish activists who had been put into another barbed wire cage, but there were also a number of Arabs among them, as well as some Germans who were suspected of being spies. On the day of our arrival some of the Jewish activists were still working in the bakehouse. They were mostly young men who tried to encourage us and to cheer us up.

The rations were wonderful. Breakfast was a feast and included fresh bread, margarine that tasted like butter, eggs, marmalade, oranges and tea. There was a good lunch at noon and a big dinner at six in the evening. We had our first taste of "Halva". Sunny spells were punctuated by rain which would come down in torrents, drumming on the tin roof of our barrack. The sound of the sea and the sporadic lightning flashes far out to sea created an eery feeling.

I expected to hear from my brother any day, but none of his letters, food parcels or clothing ever reached me. They had all been returned, as I learned much later. We were held incommunicado, no mail was delivered and no visits from relatives or friends were permitted. When the luggage arrived at long last we settled down as best we could. We talked a lot about the "Atlantic". One of the Praguers had kept a detailed diary and he would read from it in the evenings, describing the corruption in the kitchens, the pilfering, how some people gorged themselves while others starved, how every job had its food bonus and how the remonstrations of honest people were brushed aside; while drinking water was often short and the children and the sick had to go thirsty others managed to get hot water from the kitchens for a bath. Swimming had been permitted in the harbour of Heraklion, but as the swimmers clambered back over the galley roof the water from their bodies dripped into the soup and they just laughed when the cooks cursed them.

Some of the accounts of the alleged graft in the stores may have been much exaggerated—there are two sides to the story, since it cannot be denied that those who worked hard to preserve order and discipline and who boosted morale and the will to survive also needed enough food to preserve their strength. As for the Schönbrunners, I never realised that there were so many Jews in Vienna who spoke the broadest vernacular, neither did I know that so many of the Viennese Jews whose ancestors had lived there for generations still spoke Yiddish. Some of them (presumably the ones whom the Nazis had denoted as "criminals") had been in concentration camps and had come out damaged in body and mind. If their behaviour was perhaps odd at times, this was scarcely surprising. Some young people looked upon the elderly as burdensome ballast who should not have been on the transport at all since they were unlikely to make much of a contribution to the building of the nation. It did not occur to them that some of these very same people had children in Eretz Israel whose pioneering work had created the foundations of a state in which all Jews would be welcome and where they would be able to enjoy the rights of free citizens.

The individual barracks in the camp were beginning to vie with each other in beautifying the environment. Flower beds were dug and seeds were sown. It was thought that our stay might be long and that we might only gradually be released to join our relatives, but after a stay of little more than a week the rumour of an impending deportation turned out to be true and we were told to pack. We were loaded into buses early in the morning and taken back to Haifa. Once again we passed through the lovely town and arrived at Atlit. Again our persons and the luggage were frisked and the police were unexpectedly rough in their pretended search for arms.

A street divided the camp into two parts. The survivors of the "Patria" were separated from the others by a double fence of barbed wire. As we joined the former passengers from the "Atlantic" we were presently followed by the last batch from the cannibalised ship where they had been kept ever since she had entered the port of Haifa. They were glad to be ashore at last.

Atlit camp was not nearly as neat and tidy as the camp near Akko. The footpaths were muddy and strewn with boulders. A low hill barred the view out to sea and we were not permitted to go near the beach. Fifty men had to squeeze into a barrack each of which was intended for thirty. The camp was large and there were hundreds of huts holding some 3,500 people altogether including women and children who had been segregated until then. The noise was deafening. Arab workers were reinforcing the barbed wire fencing. We were recognising friends and acquaintances on the other side and would shout across, enquiring about mutual friends.

Most of the people from the "Patria" knew of someone who had been killed. All of them had lost their luggage and they wore bits of clothing which kind people had given them. We knew that there had been some 400 people from the "Patronka" on the boat when it sunk. People had been transferred there from the "Pacific", but there were also some who had come down the Danube on the "Uranus", the "Melk" and the "Helios".

As for the "Patria", some people said that she had been blown up by the Jews themselves in a desperate attempt to sabotage the government's plan to deport them. Those aboard were all supposed to jump into the water before the explosion, but something had gone wrong with the timing. It was sad to think that precious tonnage was diverted from the war effort at a time of great need for ships in order to deport a few hundred Jewish refugees to a malaria-infested prison camp on a remote tropical island. All the more so as these people were literally within sight of their relatives and friends and could, moreover, have made a valuable contribution to the common cause.

Such news as did reach us was confusing. The Yishuv was seething with indignation and there were massive strikes. It was hoped that an amnesty would be announced for those who had committed the 'crime' of illegal entry in their desperate bid for survival. The hope lasted for less than a day. At 2 p.m. on December 8th we were officially told that only those who had been on the "Patria" would be permitted to stay. The rest of us would be deported the following day. After all that we had been through we were determined to make a desperate gesture of defiance. Some of us were over 80 years old and it was more than doubtful that they would ever see their relatives if they were now carried off to a prison on a faraway tropical island. What about the traditional right of asylum that the British were always harping on and of which they were so inordinately proud? We just couldn't believe that they could do this to us. The transport leaders who had brought us thus far resigned immediately. At the request of the camp commandant we elected a spokesman to act as a liaison officer. He was called at 4 p.m. and received orders to start packing. The luggage was to be taken to a depot before midnight and we were to get up at 5 a.m., ready for departure at six, with one piece of hand luggage and two blankets each. All protests were useless. It was the decision of the mandatory government. They were trying to spirit us away before the Yishuv could react to the fait accompli and before it could rally to our assistance. It was essential to gain time. We might be safe if we could manage to hold out until noon.

The few Jews among the police had been taken off duty. Troops with rifles and bayonets were drawn up outside the barbed wire perimeter. We decided on passive resistance. Word was passed from barrack to barrack and also to the women's compound. We went to bed naked, left our luggage unpacked and refused to get up in the morning. We were making our protest all right, but there was little doubt about the final outcome—we just weren't in a shape to take on the Palestine police. Some older people urged compliance and argued that things would be worse if we made trouble (this kind of argument has long been the subject of many a wry Jewish joke!), but the youngsters were determined to resist and to show the British that we would not go like sheep to the slaughter after suffering unspeakable hardship to get to our ancient homeland. We tried to show that we meant to stay. The British showed us in turn that they were going to have their orders obeyed.[*]

Midnight passed and the commandant announced that the luggage would be left behind unless it was produced at once. This was ignored. The night seemed peaceful enough, but there was no peace within us. Nobody slept. The bronchitis was troubling me a great deal. I had been coughing persistently for some time and was now suffering from bowel trouble as well. There were no medicines in the camp and the sick bay was only for those who were running a high temperature. I had tried unsuccessfully to see a doctor on a number of occasions, but the nurses would only let those through who were actually shaking with fever. Dr. Steinhauer told me later that I had reached the limit of endurance and could not possibly have taken any more. Coughing and shivering with cold I put on some extra underwear.

Five o'clock. Nobody stirred. Complete silence. A quarter of an hour passed, then the crunch of army boots and batons banging on the walls. Doors were thrown open amid shouting. A burly policeman kicked the bed planks from under me and pulled off the blankets. The place was a shambles in no time. As soon as the police had gone we pulled the blankets over again and listened to the commotion in the next barrack. There were screams from the women's compound. It was six.

An officer appeared and again demanded that we get dressed. The order was ignored by all except one man who had been most vociferous in urging resistance the night before. An hour had been gained, but there was still a long way to go until noon. The police returned and repeated the order which was ignored yet again. They pulled off the blankets and began to wield their truncheons. I suffered a bruised elbow which presently became very sore. A second unit arrived carrying truncheons and batons. The futility of further resistance became apparent—our hut held mostly elderly people. We dressed and started packing, but before we could finish another gang of thugs was upon us and drove us outside. I grabbed my attaché case and a couple of blankets; the rest stayed behind, but I could not have

---

[*]   Here, as well as a little later in the narrative, one can discern a disturbing parallel—though undoubtedly at a different level of viciousness—between the Nazi KZ thugs and some of the British colonial police. (RSL).

carried any more anyway. Those who were not out by then were thrown out by the scruff of the neck.

Outside baton wielding policemen chased several youngsters up the street and rained blows down upon them. The youngsters were covered in blood as they were driven back screaming. They had occupied an adjoining hut and had refused to dress; they had crept out and run all over the camp stark naked urging continued defiance. They were caught one by one and beaten up until they collapsed bleeding. Finally they were thrown back inside. Now they did want to cover themselves, but the clothes and luggage had been taken away. Barefoot, wrapped in a blanket and still bleeding they passed the women's compound and the compound of the "Patria" survivors on the way to the bus. The latter had been kept indoors throughout. The women were sobbing, but the police were having fun. They taunted us, laughed, jeered and shouted: "Look at the bloody Jews!" One man had an epileptic fit and was thrown about like a sack of potatoes.

The previous day the commandant had urged us to make up an embarkation list for two contingents so as to ensure that families were not split up. Unwilling to assist in our own destruction and determined to make the British do their own dirty work, we ignored this request. Now families and friends were split up deliberately as a punishment for disobedience. We were loaded into open lorries which were completely covered with tarpaulins, with one soldier at the front and one at the back. They looked embarrassed and offered us cigarettes. They tried to indicate that there was nothing personal, as far as they were concerned, and that they were only obeying orders. Most people ignored them. The lorries tore along the road escorted by armoured cars. It was obvious that speed was of the essence so as to create a fait accompli and to prevent the mobilisation of public opinion in an attempt to forestall any militant action on the part of the Yishuv.

Having ignored the commandant's instruction to pick up provisions we had not eaten that morning. We were wondering whether all the heroics had been worth while and whether it would not have been better to draft a protest letter designed to soften the attitude of the administration. That would have been quite futile, since the decision to deport us had come from the governor himself. Some things could have been gained by compliance at the outset: we would have left in an orderly fashion, families would not have been split up, we would have kept our belongings with us and the bullies of the

Palestine police would not have been let loose to humiliate us and to indulge their sadism. But we had scored a point of honour—at a price—and this had saved some of our self-respect. Perhaps the transport leaders should not have resigned when they did—after all, their organisational expertise had kept us going ever since Bratislava. They must have had a bellyfull by then. They had done their best, they had often been vilified, they had at times been accused of arrogance, corruption and graft and they had had little gratitude for their pains.

We arrived at the harbour and were marched into the customs hall where such luggage as we had with us was examined once again. Most of it had stayed behind but what there was was loaded onto the ships; a long time was to elapse before we could lay our hands on it. All cameras, watches, razors, metal plates, mess tins, cooking utensils and cutlery were likewise confiscated. Underwear, food and medicines, bottles and cigarettes, toilet articles (even soap and toothbrushes) were taken. Anyone who protested was roughly handled. Many people were searched twice and further items were taken away the second time. Some of the women who had got to the "Patria" before she sank had been permitted to stay, but their husbands were now being deported. We were clearly pawns in the imperial game which the British were playing in Palestine. The Balfour Declaration was forgotten. Action against the Yishuv both by the army and by the Palestine police was encouraged, never mind that Hitler was our common enemy, never mind that the Arab leaders supported the Germans and never mind that the mufti of Jerusalem was broadcasting Nazi propaganda from Berlin.

7. "Nieuw Zeeland"

The harbour area was deserted. The dockers were on strike. Two large Dutch East Indiamen lay at anchor. The ship was heavily guarded and its largely Asian crew were all dressed in white. They eyed us with curiosity. The ships were painted grey but they looked smart. We boarded the 11,000 ton "Nieuw Zeeland" and an officer checked us in as we arrived. We passed through long gangways, down some staircases and reached the hold. The ship had been converted to a troop carrier. There were luggage racks, shelves, hooks and cupboards for cutlery and crockery and the place was well lit by electricity. The central section was empty. Two large ducts were supposed to provide ventilation, but they were covered with tarpaulins. The hold was fitted with bulkheads; these were partially removed during the day to admit daylight and to relieve the stuffy atmosphere. They were re-positioned and blacked out with tarpaulins during the hours of darkness. There were tables and benches at either end which accommodated fifteen men each. The floors were covered with brown linoleum. The hammocks were hooked onto the ceiling and there were rails for the blankets. The galley and the bakehouse flanked the top of the staircase on either side. Further along were more tables and benches. The portholes afforded a view of the sea, but when they were shut and the bulkhead and tarpaulins were replaced at night it soon became unbearably hot and by the morning our blankets were soaked with sweat, even though everybody slept naked. It was sticky enough with the porthole open during the day when we walked about stripped to the waist. One had to get near a ventilation duct to obtain a breath of fresh air. Most people had the same idea. The staircases were guarded by armed police who were rough and hostile. The toilets were upstairs and could only be visited at specified times, much to the distress of those who suffered from diarrhoea. I had hoped to convalesce at my brother's apartment in Haifa, but now I was getting worse. More than four hundred people were packed into one hold. A second hold was reserved for the women and children. A number of couples were separated. Some were on different ships. It was rumoured that the

"Nieuw Zeeland" and her sister ship "Johan de Wit" were bound for different destinations. We had not been officially informed where we were being dispatched to, but some of the crew (who obviously knew) said that it was a beautiful place.

The "Nieuw Zeeland" had several hundred cabins for perhaps two thousand passengers, but they were all unoccupied except for those taken by the police escort: A peacetime cruise on this ship must have been very pleasant. For the first few days we were all confined to the hold and were unable to see much as we passed through the Suez Canal, but when we entered the Red Sea we were allowed up on deck for two hours each morning and afternoon. This was presently extended to four hours. I had only a winter suit and thick underwear. It had been cold in Atlit and all my lightweight outfit had remained behind. I borrowed some thin underpants from friends who had been lucky enough to have all their luggage with them. The poor wretches who had been taken aboard just wrapped in blankets were given some clothes by others who could spare them and also by the Dutch officers who, in marked contrast to the British, were kind and sympathetic. But once again some of our own people behaved selfishly and were slow to part with some of their surplus. My good friend Nettl wore some ladies' knickers and a blouse. I gave him a pair of galoshes which were better than no shoes at all, but which were, of course, much too big for his bare feet. It was pathetic, but the policemen thought that he looked very funny. The "Atlantic" had always been rather like a floating gypsy encampment, but no laundry was allowed to be hung up on the "Nieuw Zeeland". On the other hand, there was no pilfering from washing lines either.

The food was excellent. Three men from each table took turns to fetch the rations and to do the washing up. There was tea, porridge, fried sausages and bacon, marmalade, butter and fresh white bread for breakfast; there was meat and vegetables, dessert or stewed fruit for lunch and cheese, sausages, bread and butter for tea, but unfortunately we had to take our meals in the hellish heat of the hold.

Those who were over 50 were now permitted to sleep on deck. This was presently extended to anybody who wanted to do so and was much appreciated. People came up as soon as supper was over. Remaining partly dressed, well tucked up in a blanket and wearing a cap I was quite comfortable, even though it was a little chilly at times. We had become quite used to sleeping on bare floors long ago. The ship made steady progress. The engines were quiet and the sea was calm. The rolling was only noticeable when one looked up at the stars. We had to return to the hold at 5 am. where we stripped down to the underpants.

One night we were surprised by the sudden breaking of a rainstorm. Slow to seek shelter I was unable to reach the hold in time and got soaked to the skin. The bakehouse was busy that night and it was stuffier down there than ever. No sooner had I found a spot to stretch out when the rain became a cloudburst. Torrents of water cascaded down the stairs and I was drenched a second time. I got to the bakehouse and asked a policeman who was on guard duty to let me rest there a while. He pushed me and I skidded the length of the galley to the far end, but having worked off his aggression he paid no further attention. So I bedded down on one of the benches.

Some of us were detailed to take provisions to the stores from the refrigerated holds and they reported that everything there was spick and span. We kept our own quarters clean. This was easy because there were hoses and scrubbing brushes and plenty of hot water. The ablutions had forty wash basins and taps with fresh water, but the showers had seawater and were available for only one hour each morning for reasons that were as mysterious as those which restricted the use of the toilets to specified times. This may have amused the chief of police who was no particular friend of ours. He ordered that all the men's heads be shaved and this took two mornings. He even wanted the women to be shorn, but eventually he contented himself with having their hair cropped short. He got himself drunk and tried to force his way into a woman's cabin, but she screamed and a Dutch officer appeared. The two men began to argue and the captain was summoned. The police chief was relieved from his duties and was later handed over to the authorities in Port Louis.

Unfortunately it must be admitted that some of the women were not indifferent to the attention of the policemen. It needs a great deal of self-abasement to take up with those who had beaten up their menfolk, all for a bar of chocolate or for a packet of cigarettes, especially when food was plentiful and nobody needed to go hungry. At Christmas some of the policemen got hold of several girls and they had a noisy party. One of the drunken revellers came up among the sleepers on the deck, created a commotion and threw a glass of wine which dropped on some clothes nearby without breaking.

We had an escort of two naval vessels who were tacking incessantly. One was well ahead, the other far behind. Our ships had guns and were ready to defend themselves, but no enemy craft or airplane appeared as we passed the coast of Eritrea and rounded the horn of Africa. Sailing through the straits of Bab-el-Mandeb and along the desert coast of Arabia we passed a number of British convoys. Craggy mountain ranges rose in the distance. They looked like stage props. The landscape was a study in yellow, ochre and grey without a trace of greenery.

It became hotter and hotter. Taking a meal in the hold was sheer torture now and it became impossible to walk on deck barefoot. We reached Aden, a fine harbour flanked by steep rocks. Ships of every kind were anchored in the bay, warships, tankers, merchantmen, passenger liners that had been converted into troop carriers, sailing dinghies, motor launches and steam ferries, as well as a motley collection of local fishing barges. The town was some distance away and appeared to consist of two parts, one European, the other Arab. A narrow strip of vegetation adorned the waterfront. The "Johan de Wit" lay deep inside the bay, quite a distance away. while the "Nieuw Zeeland" remained near the port entrance. We were not allowed on deck during the three days that we spent there. Eleven days had passed since we had left Haifa. The warships returned northward to escort a convoy which included a large battle cruiser.

We were leaving the shores of Asia. Our destination was no longer a secret. We were bound for Mauritius where we were due in another six days' time. There was a swimming pool on the "Nieuw Zeeland" which we had been allowed to use on the day of the shaving of heads, but the children enjoyed the use of it every day. The Dutch officers were very friendly. They threw a party for the children and gave them chocolate, fruit and ice cream. The captain hat promised that nobody would be short of food. He had much sympathy for us and said that many Dutchmen also had had to leave their homeland. He would point out that our deportation had nothing to do with him. The ship's doctor remarked that we were lucky to go to an island which was "so much more beautiful than Palestine". The policemen who had guarded us all the way from Atlit also sang the praises of Mauritius as if they were trying to sell us a holiday cruise. They even expressed the opinion that we would surely be permitted to go to Palestine once the war was over.

Two of my fellow travellers were already planning to start a confectionery business on the island and assumed that they would be free and might even settle there permanently!

The air of the open Indian Ocean was much less oppressive than around the Red Sea even though we were getting close to the Equator. We had to stop twice as the flags of Britain and Holland dropped to half mast and the dead were lowered into the sea.

Part of the promenade deck was now open to us and we enjoyed watching the flying fishes skipping over the smooth waters. Some of the women were disporting themselves in bathing costumes which left little to the imagination and a few wore thick make-up. The officers told them in no uncertain terms that they would not be allowed to come on deck unless they were properly dressed and that bare midriffs and bikinis were not acceptable. Morale was low, but occasionally a wry joke was cracked. On December 27th a few birds were seen to hover overhead and mountains arose in the hazy distance. Presently we were able to make out the contours of a triple peak which dominated a mountain range. We were approaching St. Louis, the principal port and capital city of Mauritius. A policeman pointed towards it and said: "This is your new home."

8. Beau Bassin

Mauritius is one of the most heavily populated places in the world. A town came view. We entered the harbour and dropped anchor while the "Johan de Wit" made fast along the jetty. The vegetation is tropical and luxuriant. The mountains were green almost up to the very top. Low storage huts were strung out all along the waterfront. That night the policemen went ashore and got drunk. One of them nearly fell off the gangway on his return. Three days later we were taken off by motor launch, passed through the first class passenger section and caught a glimpse of the elegant dining room, the rich décor and the well designed furniture.

We disembarked quietly. The luggage, such as there was, was taken care of by the locals. We boarded the buses that had drawn up alongside. We saw little of Port Louis, since the port was some distance from the town. A metalled road ascended towards Beau Bassin. The natural beauty of the place was breathtaking. There were two local policemen on each coach and they were very friendly. Coloured people lined the streets of the village and threw flowers as we passed. Half an hour later we came up to a stone wall and entered a garden city with well spaced-out villas and bungalows. Presently the road made a sharp turn and we found ourselves in front of a greyish brown single-storey stone building. It was surrounded by a seven foot stone wall. The gate was guarded by bearded Sikh soldiers wearing khaki turbans. There was a group of native policemen with a wide range of skin colour and body physique. We passed along the office block and came to a gate made of stout iron bars. A policeman led us to one of two taller buildings. We stood in an enormous prison hall containing three galleries of cells. I saw an acquaintance from the "Johan de Wit" who had arrived the previous evening. He assured us that it wasn't half as bad as it looked.

Two cast iron staircases led to the gallery on either side. Two reception officer sat at a table in the centre of the hall, one checking the names and particulars, the other issuing bars of soap and prison numbers which were printed on a thin piece of cardboard. Mine was 1807.

Those under fifty were led to cells with a floor area of four by seven foot. The cells were about ten foot high and quite bare, except for a hammock. There was a one foot square ventilation hole at the top. This was covered by a wooden shutter which was hung on the outside. I was taken to a wooden hut with a corrugated iron roof which contained thirty bedsteads. I would have preferred the privacy of a cell, but I presently found myself in the company of five others whom I had known since Bratislava. There was a group of old Chasidic Jews with flowing beards who had set up an ark with a Torah scroll.

We had had no food since breakfast, but now we received some tea and a piece of bread. Next morning I awoke with a swollen face and puffed-up arms. Mosquito nets did not arrive for weeks.

The women and children were put into barracks. A high stone wall separated them from the men's compound. A massive stone building stood in each compound which was surrounded by a barbed wire fence. These were the men's and the women's sick bays. Food was given out in the hall of the main prison block. Nobody had a mess tin or a spoon. Some containers were improvised from old food cans and these were passed around. We were given fish and runner beans which had been prepared by native cooks. We ate with our fingers. The food distribution was chaotic and the size of the portions varied greatly, but considering the circumstances and our condition we could hardly be expected to be paragons of discipline and keepers of a stiff upper lip. We first had to recover both physically and psychologically.

I was in a really bad way. The cough and the diarrhoea were worse than ever. The camp food was of poor quality and totally insufficient. My weight was down to 47 kilos. The rainy season had come early and it had been pouring almost incessantly for nearly four weeks. The camp was a quagmire, mosquitos were breeding in the puddles of stagnant water and there were swarms of flies. Large quantities of insecticide had been sprayed, but it was too late to prevent the spread of malaria. Typhoid was endemic and soon became a major problem because of the open construction of the latrines. Large numbers of detainees fell sick. Fresh vaccinations were carried out, but while typhoid was being contained, so malaria spread. The sick bays were unable to hold all the patients. The commandant asked a deputation to inspect a plot of ground which had been set aside for a cemetery. Within four weeks 45 people died of typhoid fever and five coffins were carried out of the gates on one day alone.

The luggage had been put in store at the camp, but it took many weeks before it was gradually released. The locks of my suitcase had been forced by the customs in Haifa and a number of items were missing, but I was glad to get back what was left.

It was rumoured that a young man named Rabl had been involved in the "Patria" affair. This was later confirmed. I had come across the name before. If he was the same quiet and balanced young man whom I thought I remembered then it was obvious that only the most extreme desperation could have made him do such a thing. He had accepted fearful odds to escape to freedom like the rest of us. He was jailed for seven years.

Alter a fortnight I was moved to hut 7 together with five others. There was more room there, but it was so damp that our shoes and clothes became white with mildew and had to be put out to dry out in the sun whenever the tropical rain offered an hour's respite. We did not stay there long. The hut was needed as an emergency sick bay. I was moved to block B, ward 3, cell 38 a fortnight later. I was not altogether displeased to be on my own. I was now able to sleep without disturbing others with my coughing and soon got used to the hammock. My intestinal troubles, however, had got so bad that I was taken to the sick bay, which everybody dreaded.

I stayed there for a month, surrounded by typhoid patients. Several people died. One Palestine policeman was greatly praised for giving blood to save a little boy who unfortunately died nevertheless. This policeman was one of only four who had not returned to Palestine and who had stayed on the island. I owe my recovery mainly to Dr. Kummermann who eased my cough and who eventually cured me of the bronchitis.

The large space between the two prison blocks was divided into four sections. The ablutions and the toilets were situated there. Eventually the latter were rebuilt and fitted with flushing devices and mosquito netting. Everybody below the age of 35 was supposed to do some work. This was not arduous. It largely consisted of maintenance jobs and was designed to improve the prison amenities. We ran the kitchens and the bakehouse, set up a tailor's shop, a locksmith's, a joiner's, a carpenter's as well as plumbing and engineering workshops. A recreation hut was built and fitted out with a stage. Language courses in English and in Hebrew were organised and a spokesman was elected to liaise with the camp commandant. There was plenty of friction at first, but gradually a camp routine emerged and some kind of provisional normality began to establish itself. The prison gates had closed behind us for an unpredictable term, but we all live in the hope of leaving this island and of being reunited with our families in freedom.

9. Postscript

Here ends my father's account, but the story continues. Descriptions of life in refugee camps have, alas, become commonplace. Refugee camps have become the institutional garbage dumps of the twentieth century. Like the workhouses and the debtors' prisons of Charles Dickens' days their beastliness and their banality have unfortunately come to bore rather than to disturb the conscience of civilised man.

The detainees on Mauritius spent several years in the prison of Beau Bassin. Dr. Zwergbaum has documented their history. He was a young man at the time and had been a spokesman of the detainees. He settled in Israel after the war. The Mauritians themselves were friendly and generous and there are reports of many kindnesses. One of the most remarkable Mauritians was Mme. Françoise Pitot, a lady linguist who lives and works in Germany at present and who has been researching government archives for many years. She unearthed a lot of documentation about the Mauritius affair and this revealed some quite remarkably shabby actions on the part of prominent persons and government departments. Mme. Pitot has devoted her life to maintaining contact with the ex-detainees and is always most welcome when she visits them or their descendants in Israel and elsewhere. My father's good friend Dr. Heller (see later) has also written about the episode from a somewhat different angle.

As for myself, I was interned as an "enemy alien" after the fall of France and was not released from the Isle of Man until thirteen months later. I was about 19 at the time. The internees set up a school in the camp. Many distinguished scientists there were happy to teach us youngsters. When they were released many of them made notable contributions to the war effort. Some of us were able to sit the Matriculation Examination of the University of London at Douglas Art School following the University's agreement to set up an examination centre on the island for our exclusive benefit. The examination fees were very kindly paid by the International Student Service. I was lucky enough to pass this examination, which later enabled me to engage upon part-time degree studies at Birkbeck College while earn-ing a living as a laboratory assistant during the day. I first obtained an honours degree in Chemistry, then in Zoology, eventually went on to a PhD in Material Science and to Fellowships of professional institutes. I carried out industrial and academic research and development work, spent a year as a Fulbright-Hays Scholar and as a Visiting Research Associate Professor at the University of Tennessee and became a United Nations expert in which capacity I carried out academic missions in China and India. I published some fifty original papers and several scientific monographs, became a naturalised British subject, married and raised a family. But this is another story.

It was in the internment camp on the Isle of Man that I learned that my father had succeeded in escaping from the Nazis and that, although a detainee in Mauritius, he was at least safe. Indeed, we were able to write to each other, although censorship restricted both the number and the length of letters which often took many months to reach the addressee. The letters were essentially tokens of affection and were otherwise describing how father was gradually rebuilding his strength. My uncle in Haifa and we ourselves (my mother, brother and myself) were able to send him a little money from time to time. Father used this to buy extra food from the camp canteen. He kept a meticulous account of the purchases.

Father began to take an active part in the cultural life of the camp community. He appreciated good music, although he did not play an instrument himself. But his principal forte was versification, mostly (though not exclusively) of a whimsical kind. He wrote humorous poems appropriate to specific occasions. However unfunny the situation may have been at times, his verses made others laugh when they might well have felt like crying. He produced short plays for the camp theatre, both in verse and in prose, and he became immensely popular among his fellow detainees whose morale he helped to raise when their spirits were at the lowest ebb.

The next thing we heard was the devastating news that he had passed away. Our mother received an official envelope containing a printed notification from the camp administration. Father had been 59 years old. He had been in H.M. Prison of Beau Bassin for about 16 months. Mother, practical, energetic and matter-of-fact as she was, never really recovered from the blow and died five years later, aged 56.

In a wider sense, the story does have a happy ending. The refugees who had at times degenerated into an undisciplined and demoralised rabble regained their self-respect and dignity. Most of the survivors from Beau Bassin settled in Palestine after the war and helped to create and defend the modern state of Israel. Their story and the wanderings of the children of Israel in biblical times have palpable parallels. They, too, were refined in the crucible of suffering and have lived to triumph over Amalek.

Ordinary decent people do not see themselves in a heroic roll. Father certainly never thought of himself as a hero. He was a modest and scrupulously honest man. He was devoted to his family and perhaps a little sentimental at times. Above all, he was kind and gentle and therefore particularly vulnerable and ill-equipped to confront an age of barbarism. He was of the stuff of which saints are made. May he rest in peace.

It is fitting that the concluding words should belong to the man who had been his best friend at Beau Bassin. Herewith two of his letters in free translation:

Dear Mrs. Lenk and sons,

This is a most difficult letter for me. I am only getting down to writing it after learning that Prof. Dr. Robert Lenk of Haifa has given you the sad news which I had sent him by telegram. I have written another two long letters to him since. Now I must write to you about my poor dear friend's last days. His sudden passing has shaken us very badly. We wish to express our deepest sympathy in your bereavement and sorrow.

A man who carries love within him generates love in response. His love for you filled him utterly and found constant expression in his conversation and in his writings. You were the focus of his every thought. Whenever your letters arrived it was a day of rejoicing and when photographs were included his eyes would light up and he would show them around with pride. The hope of an ultimate reunion never left him up to his last moment. Thinking of you made him happy. He would talk about his business trips, his work, but most of all about the joys of homecoming, about the holidays which you had all spent together, and about the wonderful relationship which he had with his sons about whose achievements he would speak with obvious and boundless pleasure.

When the long intervals of waiting seemed endless and bleak he would occupy himself with literary creativity. The golden humour of his writings bear eloquent witness to the gentle warmth of his nature, despite the horrible things that had been done to him and which might have embittered others. His writings also include some serious material.

We were utterly stunned by his death. On Monday May 17th we sat in the garden together and he recited some of his latest verse. On Tuesday morning he showed me a little red spot which he had caused by pulling a hair out of his nose. He complained about it getting rather painful and saw a doctor who put compresses on it. When he developed a temperature in the afternoon the doctor sent him to hospital which was about five minutes' walk from the camp. Visitors were only allowed on Mondays and Thursdays, but on Wednesday I heard that he was very poorly. I rang Dr. Arnold who assured me that there was no danger. I had the opportunity of visiting him at 8 a.m. the next morning and found him in a very bad state indeed. He had become much worse during the night. Erysipelas and septicaemia had developed.

He appeared to recognise me and whispered a few words which I was unable to understand. Presently he became unconscious. He was given injections and was under constant medical supervision. The chief medical officer assured me that all that could be done had been done. Dr. Freudenheim took over the vigil towards noon, but our poor friend had passed away before I could return. He had never been aware just how seriously ill he had been and he never seemed to have suffered any pain.

The funeral had to be carried out without delay, as is customary in the tropics. We buried him on Friday, May 21st. The cemetery is rather a lonely spot, perhaps half an hour's walk to the south of the camp. Cantor Löwensohn sang and recited the prayers and Rabbi Dr. Bieler and I spoke. His grave is the 74th in our division. We intend to put up a simple but dignified stone, as is the custom here.

He left no will. There is a small amount of money which is in the keeping of the commandant at present. It will be used for the grave. We shall be making a list of his belongings. Articles of sentimental value will be taken care of until they can be sent to you in safety. The remainder is usually sold by the commandant who then remits the proceeds to the next of kin. I shall be looking after his correspondence and his literary works. I am having the most important of them copied, so that nothing should be lost. I shall do all I can to act in your interest. Mail takes a very long time and this makes communications difficult, but do please let me know what your particular wishes are.

To you, Mrs. Lenk, and to your dear sons I can only say this: The bitter suffering of these last few years have broken a weak body, but it never broke the noble spirit that dwelled within. This spirit cements ever more firmly the bond of love and union at a higher level. No physical suffering has ever clouded his thinking or soured his personality, nor did hope ever give way to despair for any length of time. As he rests in peace and serenity no danger can threaten him any more, no cruel fate can touch him and no disappointment can mock or torment him. He lives on in our thoughts and in our hearts.

As for ourselves, we must grieve in silence. Life goes on, the gaps close. It is always the best who die an untimely death. May you have strength to bear the blow and have long life to honour his memory.

With heartfelt condolences and kind regards,

Yours most sincerely,

Alfred Heller.

My wife joins me in my condolences. She cannot write herself because she is down with the malaria.

From: Dr. Alfred Heller, No. 1663, P.O. Box 1000, Mauritius, March 4th, 1944.

Dear Mrs. Lenk,

A few days ago I received your and your sons' very kind letter dated November 27th. I hasten to reply as best I can.

I am not aware that your husband had been suffering from heart trouble. He never complained about any such thing, but the exertions of the abortive Yugoslav venture may quite possibly have affected his lungs and ever since Bratislava his bronchitis had troubled him greatly. He was susceptible to colds and was careful to avoid them, but this was not easy...

He never spoke about any allegedly existing opportunity of getting into Switzerland. I am sure it didn't exist and I base this on my own experience. I have the impression that he tried everything that was humanly possible, but he had just been singularly unlucky. Of course, it is possible that the many successive disappointments made him misjudge situations and fail to grasp a genuine opportunity when it did come his way. In the introduction to the memoirs of his journey he tried to show how a whim of fortune can confound all expectations. One of his most tragically missed opportunities was the failure to report sick at Atlit. A day's delay, perhaps even a few hours and he would have been allowed to stay with Dr. Lenk in Haifa. There were several of us who made it that way. I myself just barely caught a glimpse of my son-in-law before they took me away.

I do not know whether you have received any further communication or any accounts from the camp commandant at Beau Bassin since I last wrote. If you have not, then I advise you to write to the area commandant. Some of your late husband's belongings have been sold, others, including his watch and a few articles of sentimental value are being kept locally. We have his attaché case and all his correspondence. I have taken care of his writings which include essays, poems and sketches and 1 shall send these on to you at the first opportunity that enables me to do so safely.

His grave is covered with a slab of concrete and there is a headstone. The graves are all identical here, but I insisted on the concrete slab for the sake of better preservation. The inscription is in German and in Hebrew, as is usual here. I am getting it photographed and I shall send you a picture in due course.

Many thanks for your generous offer. I do appreciate it as a token of good will, but my children in Haifa are sending me whatever I need, so please do not bother with anything. However, seeing that you are so exceedingly kind, may I ask you to contact a close lady friend of my wife's who lives in England and who lost her husband shortly after arriving there. We have not heard from her for a long time and our many letters apparently failed to reach her...

My particular thanks to you, young Messrs. Lenk, for your very kind lines. Your father spoke of you many, many times with pride and joy and whenever he heard how well you were getting on. His only wish was a good life for you all. No doubt you will ease your mother's sorrow and continue to live in fraternal concord. Your father never imagined that you would have to face the future without him around to ensure your wellbeing which he saw as the supreme purpose of his life. The memory of his honesty, his righteousness, his compassion and his love will sustain you.

If there is anything I can do, please do not hesitate to let me know. My wife is unfortunately still suffering from malaria, but she joins me in sending you our very best regards and good wishes.

Yours most sincerely,

Alfred Heller.

Comments from the Press
"King opposed aliya"

The following is reprinted from the "Jewish Chronicle"
dated December 23rd, 1977.

Jewish Chronicle Reporter

Reference to the message sent to Lord Halifax by King George VI in March, 1939 relating to the number of Jewish refugees entering Palestine, was made by Mr. Martin Gilbert, a fellow of Merton College, Oxford, and Sir Winston Churchill's biographer, when he addressed a joint meeting of the B'nai B'rith Leo Baeck (London) lodges and the Society for Jewish Study, at Hillel House, Euston.

Mr. Gilbert was giving the annual Leo Baeck Memorial Lecture on "Britain, Palestine and the Jews, 1939-40, some new documents and some old reflections."

The president of the Leo Baeck Lodge, Mr. Werner M. Lash, was in the chair.

Mr. Gilbert said that the King's message, sent from Buckingham Palace, stated that he had heard that "a number of Jewish refugees from different countries were surreptitiously getting into Palestine." He was glad to think that steps were being taken to prevent these people from leaving their countries of origin.

Mr. Gilbert quoted an extract from a letter which Mr. Neville Chamberlain had written to his sister following a deputation from senior British Jews who had pleaded for a few more visas for Jews wishing to enter Palestine.

Mr. Chamberlain, he said, had expressed his basic dislike for aspects of Nazi persecution, and then he added: "At the same time Jews are not lovable people. I do not care for them myself."

Mr. Gilbert's lecture was mainly devoted to the struggle by Jews to get immigration to Palestine accepted by Britain and the British Government's difficulties in that respect. At that time the Foreign Office took the view that to contemplate a Jewish majority in Palestine would antagonise the Moslems.

One Foreign Office comment was that if the British solution displeased the Jews, they would let off "a lot of hot air", but if it displeased the Arabs, they would act.

In the House of Commons on June 5, 1939, however, Mr. Josiah Wedgwood declared that the policy pursued by the Government and by Mr. Malcolm MacDonald, the then Colonial Secretary, particularly, was worthy of Hitler and the Middle Ages. He added that if the Government succeeded in stopping "illegal" immigration, it would stink in the nostrils of posterity.

(The following article is reprinted from the "Jewish Chronicle"
of March 6, 1981)

Bevin and the Jews

By S.J. Goldsmith

ERNEST BEVIN was born on March 7, 1881. For the past few months the press has carried both articles and letters offering suggestions for a suitable way to mark the centenary - monuments, foundations, scholarships, festive gatherings. The trade unions are in the forefront of the Bevin sponsors, but they are not the only ones. The anniversary is being marked in this country as a national event: few British statesmen have been thus celebrated.

As far as the British are concerned, Ernest Bevin may have done enough to deserve all this. But it should not blind us to the fact that he was the man who tried to destroy the Jewish National Home. He did not succeed, but he had a good try.

Bevin made his contribution - and a significant one, at that - to the struggle for a decent standard of life for the British working man. He successfully mobilised British manpower during the Second World War. He helped to establish Nato. He grasped the importance of the Marshall Plan. Whether he was a great Foreign Secretary is another matter. A great Foreign Secretary is one who succeeds in what he sets out to accomplish. Bevin mostly failed, and he failed in some major issues. He did not prevent the Cold War. He did not stop the Jews establishing their State. He did not even retain the friendship of the Arabs. And he was confused over Korea.

I have some "proprietary rights" in the Bevin saga. It was to a fair and straightforward question of mine - at a press conference in London in October, 1945 - that he made his first public anti-Semitic remark, and after that we knew where he stood (or at least some of us knew).

I was still a war correspondent in uniform, having come over from the Continent for just a few days. My question related to UNRRA (United Nations Relief and Rehabilitation administration). I had not mentioned Jews, but Bevin jumped up and screamed in anger: "Everybody will be taken care of, but the Jews must not push themselves to the head of the queue."

That sort of language would have been bad enough any time, but this was only a few months after the liberation of the concentration camps. The stark horror of the Nazi order was not yet fully comprehended by the free world.

Bevin was not, of course, the type of anti-Semite who breaks Jewish-owned windows; if you catch that type, you know what to do. Bevin was the "Hamanic" type, the sort who attempts to undermine the very existence of the Jewish people. Such anti-Semites are, of course, far more pernicious than the hooligans. Ben-Gurion once remarked (in my hearing) that we had learned how to deal with that type, too, but the price had been high.

Bevin himself left no diaries or private papers; all that remained were a few barely legible and ungrammatical notes. According to Lord Butler, Bevin could neither read nor write.

But the documents opened to the public after thirty years were written by civil servants, who could read and write well. They are unmistakable, and spine-chilling, in their callousness and inhumanity. They also show clearly that Bevin had the enthusiastic support of his Prime Minister Clement Attlee.

At Bevin's instigation attempts were made by British diplomats - in some cases against their will and better judgement - to persuade European governments to stop Holocaust survivors leaving European countries "lest they try to proceed to Palestine". The return of concentration camp survivors to Germany, the "Struma", the "Patria", the Cyprus camp - are all recorded history. Let it be said that many Englishmen are deeply ashamed of these incidents, as they are of other incidents in their history.

In November 1948 the Cabinet considered the situation in "Palestine". By then the Jewish State had been established, in the wake of a two-thirds majority resolution of the United Nations. By then the Israelis had shown that they had no intention of letting the Arabs push them into the sea. By then the United States, the Soviet Union and a host of other states had recognised Israel both de jure and de facto.

Bevin was still dealing with "Palestine". Fears were expressed in the Cabinet that "the Jews are likely to attack Transjordan". A suggestion was put forward - it is not known by whom - that RAF units be sent to give cover to the Jordanian army. Another suggestion was put forward: a direct British invasion of "Palestine" - in other words, a war between Britain and Israel.

The Cabinet Papers available are not word-for-word minutes of the proceedings, but we know very well about Bevin's obsession with "Palestine", and his role in these suggestions. Attlee was, as usual, hostile to Israel, but rational. In the end, neither suggestion was acted upon. It was obvious that such ideas, if made public - even as ideas, let alone practical propositions - they would cause a public outcry at home and abroad, especially in the United States. It was also quite clear to the military experts that Britain lacked the forces to ensure a quick victory.

Bevin also expressed the view, at a Cabinet meeting, that "the Jewish State will soon collapse because of internal squabbles." So much for the vision and foresight of a "great Foreign Secretary". So much, too, for the judgement of the Foreign Office officials, who fed Bevin with information and assessments.

Bevin himself could not find Israel on the map, but the Foreign Office "experts" had no notion of the Jewish character, or of the roots the Jews had by then struck in Eretz Israel. This, 30 years after the Balfour Declaration, 27 years after Mandatory rule over Palestine, and nearly 70 years after the establishment of the first colonies in the Holy Land.

Bevin had the "scholarly" backing of the then Colonial Secretary, Arthur Creech Jones. Creech Jones had started as a friend of Zionism, but he was a weak and pitiful character.

What of British Jews and Bevin? The Zionists had no influence whatever by then. Bevin had created an abyss between himself and Zionism. The Board of Deputies kept on protesting vehemently, but its influence was (and remains) confined to home affairs.

Ordinary Jews protested, marched and were not afraid to criticise Bevin and the Government as a whole. Bevin's response was: "The Jews were upset once before, during an election, and I went down to the East End and fixed it up with them."

Do we forgive Bevin his anti-Semitism? No more so than we forgive Dostoyevsky, T.S. Eliot, Ezra Pound. They, after all, left a bigger impact on the human mind and human spirit than Ernest Bevin. We do not have to falsify history, and overlook Jewish suffering, for the sake of Ernest Bevin's soul.

The late Richard Crossman wrote that Bevin "made peace between Jews and Arabs impossible for ever". There is no such thing as "forever" in politics, but Bevin did both the Jews and the Arabs incalculable harm. And perhaps the Arabs paid an even higher price than did the Jews.

John Brown may be buried, but his soul goes marching on. Likewise with Ernest Bevin.

(The following is reprinted from the "Jewish Chronicle" of January 8, 1993)

Obedient servants

Writer Julia Pascal relates how research for her play about a Jewish deportee from wartime Guernsey gave a shocking insight into past horrors.

Theresa Steiner seems to have been an escapee from a wealthy Viennese family who had a textile business. She came to England in 1938, fleeing Hitler. She found work as a nanny, looking after the two daughters of a Beckenham dentist. When war was declared in September 1939 the dentist's family fled to Guernsey in the mistaken notion that they would escape bombing. By June 1940, after the fall of France, it was clear that the Germans were going to land on the Channel Islands. Hitler wanted the psychological boost of having invaded part of Great Britain.

Before the invasion the British government decided to remove all army personnel and give the Channel Islanders the choice of evacuation or occupation. The dentist and his family were allowed to leave, but Guernsey's chief of police, William Sculpher, refused to allow Theresa to go with them. Why did Sculpher take the unusual step of forbidding Theresa Steiner's departure even before the German invasion? There was no legal reason for him to do so. Was he an anti-Semite who knew he could use Steiner (whose passport had been stamped with a "J" by the Austrian authorities) to ingratiate himself with the régime? Nobody knows. He died in 1957.

When I arrived on the island three years ago to research my play about Theresa I was introduced to a Mr. X who asked me to conceal his identity. He allowed me access to the secret wartime documents, among them the ingratiating letters from the island's then bailiff, Victor G. Carey, to the Gestapo. I was profoundly shocked on reading this material. Carey documented all the Jews who lived or had lived on the island. Their property was evaluated. Theresa Steiner's wage as an auxiliary nurse in the local hospital was noted, as was that of fellow-Viennese worker - Nurse Auguste Spitz. A third woman, an agricultural student from Reading University, Marianna Grünfeld, is also repeatedly mentioned in the letters.

Again and again as Carey - and Sculpher - betray the whereabouts and circumstances of Guernsey's Jews, they tell the Gestapo that they have "the honour to be your obedient servant." Spitz, Steiner and Grünfeld did not hide their Jewish identity but there were several others named, including Annie Wranowsky, who claimed gentile descent. Nationalities were also referred to frequently. Annie Wranowsky appears as both German and Czech. Elizabeth Duquemin (sometimes called Duquemin) and Elda Brouard are stated to be British and thought to have been originally foreign nationals married to British men.

Mr. X took me to the hospital where Theresa worked. Part of her job was nursing the syphilitic prostitutes brought over from France to service the German soldiers in the Nazi camp of Alderney. The atmosphere in the island was extraordinary. Guernsey looks like rural Ireland except for the presence of great concrete fortresses and the terrible underground hospital built by slave labour. This is another aspect which has been concealed. Guernsey people saw lines of men, thin as skeletons, working to construct these edifices for the Germans. Most of these wretches, as in neighbouring Jersey and Alderney, were Russians, East Europeans, German anti-Nazis and French Jews.

It has been alleged that island collaborators helped the Gestapo set up these slave labour forces but, to date, no British government has expressed any interest in finding out who these collaborators were. On Guernsey itself, any mention of the war is greeted with great reticence.

One of the doctors who worked with Theresa (again someone who wishes to remain anonymous told me: "Those men should have been hanged for their war crimes. Instead, one of them was honoured."

While Inspector Sculpher was guilty of preventing Theresa's departure and therefore facilitated her death in Auschwitz, the greatest responsibility lies with bailiff Victor Carey. Liberation film shows him being knighted by the Queen Mother as if he were a war hero. Today his grandson, Vic Carey, is

the Island's deputy bailiff. The Carey's dynastic presence is not altogether popular. One Guernsey dissenter remarked to me: "Power is centred within nine key families, the Carey family at the head."

The island's wartime government (except for one protester) agreed to accept the Nuremberg Race Laws. Consequently, Guernsey's Jewish shops were daubed with anti-Semitic slogans and Jews were forbidden to go to cafés, cinemas or sit on park benches.

In addition to Carey and Sculpher, a Methodist minister, the Rev John Leale, president of the island's controlling committee, is also implicated in the betrayal of Guernsey's Jews. In November 1940 Leale passed on the names of the hunted Jews on the very day they were requested by the Gestapo.

In Guernsey Theresa Steiner lived under Nazi occupation for the second time in her life. Later she was murdered in Auschwitz with Auguste Spitz and Marianna Grünfeld. I heard talk of how other islanders were deported with the three Jews but that Spitz, Steiner and Grünfeld were isolated. They spent a night in a convent in Rennes before going to the French transit camp at Drancy. Serge Klarsfeld's files show their admittance to Auschwitz in September 1942.

When I asked some of my Guernsey contacts - supposed friends of Theresa - whether they had ever considered hiding her I was met with amazed looks. The thought had clearly never entered their heads. Others, with whom the past still rankles, reacted much more strongly. Maurice Kirk, a former vet, was so incensed by what he described as the current Guernsey government's autocracy that, when summoned to court on a minor driving offence, he appeared in Nazi uniform, claiming that "the jackboot has never left this island. It has just changed uniform."

I experienced a certain amount of resistance to my writing a play on the subject. Some Jews in Britain were against my revealing the secret British collaboration. But when one of Victor Carey's grandsons, based in London, came to see a performance of "Theresa" at the Spiro Institute's Garage Theatre in West Hampstead, he told me that there were even more Jews betrayed than I had discovered. After the war, he said, "the British government did not know whether to hang Carey or knight him." It seems somebody decided that a knighthood and a cover-up were best for British interests.

Marianna's Grünfeld's surviving cousin, Ernst Grünfeld, and his wife Erika, kindly sponsored a tour of "Theresa" to Germany. We performed it once in the former concentration camp of Breitenau; at Kassel University - where our posters were defaced - and in small studio centres in Frankfurt. The critics' response was tremendous and a special week at Heidelberg University could not satisfy demand. Often, at the end of a performance, there was a great silence followed by sobbing. German young people were as moved by the experience as Jewish survivors were in London. "Theresa" ran for two years in London (with strong support from the London Bor-

ough of Camden), in France and in Germany. Critics and audiences were unanimously warm . We played at the Lilian Baylis Theatre in Sadlers Wells, Islington and to predominantly black audiences at Oval House, Kennington who related to the experience as if it were their own. At the Garage Theatre the Spiro Institute emphasised the educational aspect of the work. Nitza and Robin Spiro asked the company to stay behind after each performance to talk with the audience. We found many survivors keen to relate their own experiences. Many young people were stunned by a part of British history about which they had never learned in school.

We were banned in Guernsey. The truth, it seems, was too hard to face.

Why did I - why do I - feel so strongly connected to Theresa Steiner? Although I was born five years after the war I felt she could have been me. Somehow I feel I owe her the homage of recognition. Thanks to her I have written a trilogy of plays about surviving the Holocaust: "Theresa", "A Dead Woman on Holiday" and a version of the "Dybbuk". As I write this an old man calls me out of the blue. He has a Viennese accent. It is her brother, Professor Carl Steiner. He escaped via Shanghai and ended up in Montreal. He is delighted that the play has been written about his lost sister. He never knew what became of her. We will meet and talk, sharing our knowledge of this talented young girl, brutally gassed because of British collaboration. I will listen to his story and learn about Theresa Steiner's early life in Vienna. And then I'll consider reviving the play.

GUERNSEY'S SHAME

Vic Carey, Will Sulpher, John Leale,
Is Guernsey still proud of your deal
With those whom you served with such zeal?

Or have you John Leale,
Messrs Sulpher and Carey
Met the ghosts of the girls
You denounced?
Have you ever given
The slightest expression
Of the guilt on your conscience?
Or penned a confession
After labouring mightily
And with zealous devotion
With other grand notables
Of your domain
Who shared with such ardour
The "Honour to be
The Obedient Servants"
(The records agree)
Of the enemies of your sovereign,
For which somewhat later
A fulsome citation
Betokened the thanks
Of your king and your nation?

Your hands remained clean
And unsullied with red
For what are six girls
Among six million dead?
Theresa, Marianne, Auguste
And Annie, Elizabeth, Elda,
To be sure you remember them well!
Though they're only six souls
Among more than six million
Whose tumbrils were rumbling
With death riding pillion.

But now is the time
To unbury a crime
Which the dead cannot tell.,
While most of your neighbours
Who knew very well
Averted their eyes
And showed neither pity
Nor shame or surprise,
So that to this day
A squalid disgrace
Disfigures the face
Of the island race.

R.S. Lenk, 1993

(The following leading article is reprinted from the "Jewish Chronicle" of
January 8, 1993)

One plus one plus one

The facts - no less stark for having spent 47 years locked in official archives - are these: Four eminent citizens of Guernsey, two of them were subsequently knighted, helped Nazi officers track down at least three foreign-born Jews who were then deported and killed. The issues raised, the current bailiff of Guernsey suggested this week, are more complex. The Germans were an occupying power, determined to get what they wanted and ready to use force if they didn't. They had denied the island legislature's "responsibility for the fate of aliens, including the three Jewish women of German birth." Besides, the island's government was preoccupied with doing all it could to buffer the effects of occupation on the rest of Guernsey's citizens. "Requests made by the Germans .. were in practice peremptory demands. Refusal was not possible, as to do so would only have brought reprisals on a helpless population." Similar arguments have been made, in different languages from different corners of the territories occupied by Hitler, to explain complicity in the eventual murder of millions of innocents by the Third Reich. Equally familiar have been the arguments for post-war secrecy and silence; the need to heal the wounds of history or - more recently, in the debate over the war crimes legislation in the British Parliament - to spare frail old men the needless pain and media attention of facing trial.

The challenge faced by those under Nazi occupation was huge, with each action or decision inevitably overshadowed by the threat of death for oneself, and others. It was a test of human fibre unimaginable for those who did not have to confront it. But to argue for secrecy and silence - or for a statute of limitations on the "little" complicities which made the huge crime possible - is wrong on many counts. The most obvious, perhaps, is that silence belittles the terrible price paid by Hitler's victims. It also blurs the distinction between good and evil that is the litmus test of civilised society. That distinction is critical now. It is not just a matter of philosophy, but of life and death: For Turkish "guest workers" burned alive as many Germans, at least initially, stood by; or for Muslims" ethnically cleansed", then brutalised in the camps of Bosnia. The current authorities in Guernsey are to be praised for releasing this week's documents, even if in part, no doubt, because the officials concerned are no longer alive. The British government and monarchy now face a challenge of their own. They should answer it, first by stripping the honours bestowed on the officials who helped the Nazis locate their victims .. Whitehall should release other papers relating to the war, notably files concerning Alderney's Nazi labour camp. Efforts should also be made to widen current war crimes investigations to include possible suspects in Guernsey, or Alderney, who may still be alive.

The point is not vengeance, but justice; not a witch-hunt, just an investigation of any evidence that suggests a genuine basis for prosecution. The most compelling arguments for this come not from London, not from politicians or pundits, but from the thousands of people who did risk their lives to save others: the mass of ordinary Danes, for instance, who conspired to save all but several hundred of the country's Jews; a small Calvinist community in north-eastern Holland which hid hundreds from deportation; or a simple sergeant-major in the German army named Hugo Armann (cited in a powerful book published last year by JC contributor Eric Silver for having saved Jews from murder squads). Accepting an honour in Israel he remarked: "I did little," but added: "If many had done little, it would have added up to much." Indeed, one risk in reading the Guernsey papers is to forget how greatly "little" numbers matter. An equally remarkable book of individual wartime "memories" compiled by New York Times writer Judy Miller concludes: "Abstraction is memory's most ardent enemy. It kills because it encourages distance, and often indifference. We must remind ourselves that the Holocaust was not six million. It was one, plus one, plus one ..."

The following article has been reprinted from the "Jewish Chronicle" of
January 29, 1993.

History Lessons

*Vernon Bogdanor, Reader in Government at Oxford University and Advisor
on their new constitutions to the new Hungarian, Czech and Slovak governments believes anti-Semitism to be a thing of the past ... present and future.*

There have been, as everyone
knows, anti-Semitic outbreaks in Germany. But there is no need to worry.
The German government has made it
clear that it stands four-square with the
Jewish community in stamping out
racism. The Minister of Justice assured a Jewish meeting in the name of
his government that the latter shares in
the sense of outrage. Fortunately, in
the most recent federal elections the
leading antisemitic party has secured
little more than 2% of the vote. There
is no danger.

There is just one problem. The
above refers not to events in 1992, but
in 1928. The anti-Semitic party which
had gained just over 2% of the vote was
the Nazi party which came to power in
Germany less than five years later.

After the murder in 1922 of Walter
Rathenau, Germany's Jewish foreign
minister, vast marches were organised
throughout the country. But the soli-
darity among anti-racists and between
Jew and non-Jew in the end counted
for nothing.

All too often Jews and others have
argued that European anti-Semitism is
a phenomenon of the past, something
that could not recur in a truly demo-
cratic state such as the Weimar Republic. After the Second World War the

Holocaust was said to have inoculated
European society against anti-Semitism.
But the growth of anti-Semitism cannot
be dismissed simply as the work of hoo-
ligan elements. In Germany most of the
attacks have come from the East. Yet the
Institute of Jewish Affairs' 1991 report
on anti-Semitism shows that antisemitic
attitudes are actually stronger in the prosperous West where between 12 and 17%
- i.e. at least 7.5 million people - could be
classified as "definitely antisemitic"
while in the East it was only 3-7%. In
France around one-fifth of the population "rather" or "totally" agreed that
there were too many Jews there, though
Jews constitute only 1% of the population, roughly the same as German Jews
before Hitler.

Of course "Bonn is not Weimar", as
the German Ambassador recently declared. Bonn is not Weimar as it was
after 1929, but is it Weimar as it was in
1928 or 1922 when society's condem-
nation of anti-Semitism couldn't have
been stronger? Some, without quite re-
alising what they are doing attribute to
Jews themselves some indirect responsibility for anti-Semitism in the past. I
have heard a prominent rabbi assert that
Jews are no longer passive victims. But
nor were they in the 1920's and 1930's.
Each generation has blamed Jews of a

past era - whether the Middle Ages, the 1890's or the 1930's - for allowing themselves to be victims. Often Jewish leaders put their faith in education or the law. Yet, this too has proved ineffective. Banning the Nazis allowed them to assume the mantle of martyrdom.

In the 1920's the German *Zentralverein* published endless texts on the contribution that Jews had made to German civilisation, the number of Jews killed in the First World War, etc. But anti-Semitism cannot be defeated by rational argument, neither does one antisemitic outbreak inoculate Europe against another. The Dreyfus affair did not inoculate Europe against the Kishinev pogrom of 1903, Kishinev did not inoculate against the Ukrainian pogrom in 1920 and that in turn did not inoculate Europe against the Holocaust.

The truth is there are no new strategies for fighting anti-Semitism that have not been tried in the past and failed. It is because anti-Semitism lies so far beyond the assumptions of liberalism that decent people underestimate its dyna-mism. If we are honest we have to say that we do not know why anti-Semitism is so pervasive, nor whether or when it will again assume dynamic proportions. This means that Jewish organisations should re-examine their strategies for dealing with it.

There is of course one difference between the situation now and that of the inter-war years or the 1890's - and that is the existence of a Jewish state within which the Jews can live without depending on the goodwill of others or the special protection of the law. Today, by contrast with the years before 1948, Jews remain a threatened minority by choice and not by compulsion.

To suggest that Jews on the Continent might enjoy a more secure future in Israel than in their own countries might seem to be a counsel of despair. And yet, if one asks the question - can the liberal decent-minded governments of Continental Europe *guarantee* that their Jewish citizens will be able to live in safety for the foreseeable future - the only honest answer is they cannot.

Three English Poems

By Rudolf S. Lenk

1. THE SURVIVOR

I see him in reflective mood
Survey the statues in the park
As if departed spirits could
Assuage the sorrow in his heart.

He is a dead man on recall
Who raises the observer's doubt
Of whether he survived at all
While others perished round about.

A gentle breeze, a swaying leaf
Presaging long denied relief
Competes with nightmares ages back.
Time failed to pacify the grief
As history rewinds the track
And plays old sounds and pictures back.

And so the dross of days drools on
Like poorly fashioned pearls of paste
And unexcited, unexcused
He sits bemused and unamused
Forever in reflective mood.

Reluctantly he plays his part
Untutored in the actor's art
Still waiting that oblivion would
Assuage the sorrow in his heart.

(July 1991)

2. The silent stage

The stage is set, but strangely still
With no performance due to start,
With none to witness or display
The magic of the Thespian art,
As if they all had walked away
Without a whisper or a tear
And nevermore to reappear
To stage the play another day.

Although the props are still around
There is no gesture and no sound,
Because the gods who plundered all
The planet's wealth without recall
Have brought about their own demise
For they wrought death in paradise.

(August 1992)

3. The Epitaph

Behold, here lies the Naked Ape,
The fool who thought he could escape
The ultimate retaliation
For atavistic gene mutation
And Nature's reckless exploitation.
His search for God could only find
A supercopy of his kind
Within a recess of his mind,
A spectre which survived to set
An epitaph proclaiming that:
The Age of Man, the self-styled Master
Has proved to be a grand disaster,
A short, but ghastly aberration
Of Time's perspective of creation.

(August 1992)

Poems in German

Sinaifahrt

Ist man an Israel's Nordseeküste
Bedient man sich des Schiffs der Wüste.
Die Trugoase vor mir gaukelt
Wenn sich das Tier im Trabe schaukelt.

Seekrankheit nehm ich gern in Kauf
Wenn ich verfolg' der Zeiten Lauf
Und Stellen finde (die markierten)
Wo meine Ahnen exodierten.

Kamelgeruch ist zu ertragen
Wenn Wüstenberge vor mir ragen
Wo Israel in alten Tagen
Gesetzestafeln, sozusagen
Empfangen aus des Herren Hand,
In Obhut nahm, um so auf Erden
Ein auserwähltes Volk zu werden.

Wenn ich das klare Wasser seh
Das Gott uns gab in Meribeh,
Von Moses aus dem Fels geschlagen
Dann will ich wohlgemut ertragen
Ein wund Gesäß für dieses Wunder
Statt Autofahrt auf Rädern runder.

Wohlan, du buckliges Gerippe,
Erhebe deine Oberlippe,
Setz Segel in den Wüstensand
Und führ mich in das öde Land
Das meine Väter durchmarschierten
Eh' sie in K'naan sich etablierten!

(Dezember 1977)

Deutschland

Deutschland, Deutschland - Kantland, Meerland,
Waldland, Seeland, Friedland, Wehrland,
Heidland, Kahlland,
Berg- und Tal-land
Weidland, Wiesen,
Zwerge, Riesen,
Moorland, Torfland,
Stadt- und Dorfland,
Diktaturland, Land der Knechte,
Land der freien Menschenrechte,
Land der Recken, Land der Geister,
Land der Gilden und der Meister,
Land der fahrenden Gesellen,
Waidmannsland und Hundebellen,
Land der Junker und der Schützen,
Fritzen und Studentenmützen,
Land von Fleiß und von Genie,
Wissenschaft und Industrie,
Heimatliches Kunst- und Tonland,
Fremd- und Gastarbeiterwohnland,
Land der Freundschaft und der Liebe,
Acker der perversen Triebe,
Land des Friedens, Land des Bauens,
Land des Krieges, Land des Grauens,
Land der Dichter, Land der Denker,
Land der Richter, Land der Henker,
Land des Dunkels, Land der Lichter,
Land verschwommener Gesichter,
Land der Weber, Land der Hämmer,
Land der Not und Land der Schlemmer,
Land des Biers und Land des Weines,
Land der Elbe und des Rheines,
Land von Burgen und von Ahnen,
Zäher Fluß auf Autobahnen,
Kreuzungspunkt auf breiter Spur
Europäischer Kultur.

Was uns trennt und was verbindet
Sich dort nunmehr wiederfindet,
Denn es ist auf kleiner Leinwand
Aller Menschen Abel-Kain-Land,
Aller Menschen Mein-und-Dein-Land.

(März 1980)

Elbequelle

Als sechzehnjähr'ger Junggeselle
Da stand ich an der Elbe Quelle;
Der Weiher füllte sich zum Rande
Und ihm entfloß im Silberbande
Ein klarer Bach; auf kühlem Steine
Erglitzert er im Sonnenscheine.

Als wir dem Isertal entstiegen
War schwerer Tau noch auf der Halde.
Wir sahen Rochlitz vor uns liegen,
Textilfabrik, die Brücke, Ziegen,
Den Aussichtsturm am Rand vom Walde
Gebaut für steten Späherblick -
Wie nutzlos war er dennoch balde
Zum Grenzschutz dieser Republik!

Beim Heimgang schwand der Sonnenschein,
Ein Unwetter es brach herein,
Ein Jahr darauf und dieses Land
Befand sich in Tyrannenhand
Und die mich eingeladen hatten
Verschwanden in das Reich der Schatten.

Verklungen ist des Pöbels Johlen,
Von Henlein's Horden keine Spur,
Doch jetzt gebietet unverhohlen
In Böhmen, Mähren, wie in Polen
Die Linksfaschistendiktatur.
Im Bann der fremden Heeresmacht
Kein Prager Frühling mehr erwacht.

Wie bist du, Böhmen, doch so schön -
Welch großes Leid hast du geseh'n!

Heut steh ich - bin ich noch derselbe? -
Am andern Ende dieser Elbe.
Gut vierzig Jahre sind verflossen,
Der Böhmerwald ist mir verschlossen -
Doch tief im Herzen glänzt die Helle
Des Sommertages an der Quelle.

(Hamburg, Mai 1979)

Bergen Belsen

Was habe ich gelernt?
Die alte und die neue Welt,
Die noch in ihren Angeln hält,
Die kenne ich, nichts ist entfernt.
Doch ihr, die Fragen an mich stellt -
Ich kann euch nichts erklären,
Kein Dogma kann ich lehren,
Denn ich bin selber immer nur
Ein suchender auf fahler Spur.
Was weiß ich schon? Ich bin ein Wand'rer -
Derselbe stets und stets ein and'rer.

Woher? Wohin? Das macht mir wenig Kummer -
Man kommt wohl vielerorts zurechte,
Die Erde nährt uns überall,
Die Rast ist süß in manchem Stall,
Ein warmer Platz für kalte Nächte
Gewährt dem Schläfer Ruh und Schlummer.
So danke ich des Zufalls Laune
Die mich bewahrt von jenem Zaune
Und daß ich niemals Hunger litt
Und frei auf freiem Boden schritt.

So kann ich es kaum fassen,
Daß das Abscheuliche
Und ewig Greuliche,
Ein ganz obszöner Fanatismus
Von Haß besessen und Sadismus
Den Menschen selbst, des Schöpfers Pracht
Millionenfach zu Aas gemacht.
Die Vorstellung im Bild erstarrt -
Ist auch das Zeugnis aufbewahrt.

Heut scheint die Sonne warm und milde
Und doch ist trostlos das Gefilde
Und nach Jahrzehnten auf der Halde,
Auf freier Flur, im lichten Walde,
Vom Frühlingsregen angerieselt
Vom Herbstens Nebel angenieselt
Hängt ein Geruch noch auf der Heide
Von Schmach und unsagbarem Leide,
Ein Seufzer, tief, aus müden Knochen,
Denn noch ist manches ungerochen.

Und wenn die Wunden auch vernarben
Für Hekatomben, die da starben
Kann es sich nie verjähren
Sie noch im Tod zu ehren.
Welch ungeheure Bürde
Ist doch des Menschen Würde!

Zum unvergeßlichen Gedächtnis
Zu aller Lebenden Vermächtnis,
Zur Mahnung künftiger Geschlechter
Sei dieser Ort ein treuer Wächter.
Vergiß nie, Pilger: Diese Stelle
War seinerzeit ein Tor der Hölle.

(Hamburg, Juni 1979)

Ohlsdorf

In Ohlsdorf dort wohnen Legionen von Toten
In unwiderruflichen Aufgeboten.
Die Hekatomben von bleichen Gebeinen
Sich unter der Erde nun friedlich vereinen.
In Schattenalleen
Von tausend Armeen
Gewichtiger Bürger und greiser Matronen
Da ruhen auch Krieger von vielen Nationen;
Die freundliche Milde
Der breiten Gefilde
Verwischt auch die Grenzen der Religionen.

Ein Kindlein, gar frühzeitig weggerafft,
Ein junger Matrose im Glanz voller Kraft,
Hier schmerzlicher Abschied, dort vorsorglich Streben
Nach Wiederverein'gung im künftigen Leben
(Denn schon ist der Name hier vorenthalten-
Der Ablebenstag ist bloß einzuschalten).
In einsamem Kummer auf einsamen Bänken
Die Menschen mit Liebe der Toten gedenken.
Sie jäten das Unkraut und pflanzen und gießen
Auf daß frische Knospen der Erde entsprießen;
So sind sie dann dennoch und trotz alter Wunden
Mit ihren Verstorbenen wiederverbunden.

Ich las der Widerstandskämpfer Zeilen,
Von mutigen Gegnern der Tyrannei.
Ich kam, bei der Denkstatt der Juden zu weilen,
Den Frieden in ihrem Gedächtnis zu teilen -
Ich fand sie nicht - doch sie war immer dabei.

Da wurde mir klar was die Toten uns lehren:
"Komm nicht, um gerade den einen au ehren,
Denn hier sind wir alle, ob arm einst, ob reich,
Wie immer gestorben, einander ganz gleich.
Erklinget wohl jenseits des Zauns das Gewimmel
Der Hansestadt freies und frohes Getümmel,
So sind wir doch allesamt bloß die Gebeine
Von Generationen im Zeitenvereine -
Und ruhest auch du einst im friedlichen Hain
So werde, wie uns, nicht zu schwer dir der Stein!"

(Hamburg, Mai 1979)

Nach Berlin!

Will Geschichte man erleben
Sollte man auf flacher Schiene
Sich der Phantasie ergeben,
Daß sie bess'rer Einsicht diene.
Dafür gibt es reichlich Muße
Bei der Fahrt im Autobusse,
Denn wenn die Gedanken schweifen
Läßt sich mancher Eindruck greifen -
Zur Vergangenheit sich paart
Fleischgeword'ne Gegenwart.

Lieber Nachbar, laß das Schwätzen,
Laß dich in der Zeit versetzen,
Dann erscheint dir auf der Strecke
Mancher renommierte Recke,
Waldleut', die die Bäume fällen,
Jäger, Hörner, Hundebellen -
Folge mir und du wirst sehen
Was in alter Zeit geschehen.

In den Sümpfen der Teutonen
Hat es Dörfer kaum gegeben,
Denn in diesen Marschregionen
Gab's ein primitives Leben,
Karge Hütten, dunkle Wälder,
Keine Straßen, keine Felder,
Nebelschwaden und Barbaren
Lockten keine Heeresscharen,
Keine Expansionsgelüste
Roms in dieser Mooreswüste,
Denn ein Zug mit Brand und Schwert
War wohl kaum der Mühe wert.

Doch im Lauf von tausend Jahren
War gewandelt das Gelände,
Nicht mehr galt der Rhein als Ende
Und als Limes der Cäsaren.
Neue Völker, neue Reiche,
Straßen, Städte, Brücken, Deiche
Und ein aufgeklärtes Denken
Sollt' fortan die Menschen lenken.

Viele sind den Weg gefahren
Seit dem Krieg von dreissig Jahren:
Wenn die Schweden einmarschieren
Hört man Landknechtstrommeln rühren
Und dann rückt der Tilly an
Zu dem Rand der Autobahn.
Später sieht die alten Fritzen
Man durch Preußens Lande flitzen
Und erkennt die Donnerblitze
Der französischen Geschütze.

Bismarck mehrt des Kaisers Ehre
Durch den Marschtritt seiner Heere:
Hoch zu Roß die Generäle,
Marschgesang aus voller Kehle.
Die geschwung'nen Säbel blitzen
Und die Pickelhaubenmützen
Nicken leicht im Trab der Pferde.
Auf der frischgepflügten Erde
Steht der Bauer in der Pfütze,
Stramm die Hand an seiner Mütze.

Doch Europa's Bürgerkriege
Brachten nichts als hohle Siege,
Hunger, Elend, Schmach und Schande,
Aderlaß der Abendlande.

Sind die Kämpfer aufgerieben,
Was ist heute noch verblieben,
Daß die Geister alter Zeiten
Noch durch diese Landschaft reiten?
Wo führt diese Straße hin?
Nach Berlin, Berlin, Berlin -
Zu der kulturellen Wiege,
Zum umstritt'nen Pfand der Kriege.

Heute ist die kahle Spur
Autobahn und Nabelschnur
Einer Weltenmetropole
Konzipiert zu Deutschlands Wohle.
Ist das große Streitobjekt
Auch ganz gründlich abgedeckt -
Fort, Vergangenheitsgedanken,
Denn jetzt öffnen sich die Schranken.
An dem Ziele angekommen
Sind die Schemen grau verschwommen -
Herzlich heißt Berlin willkommen.

(Hamburg, Juli 1979)

Osterspaziergang

Zu Heidelberg, von altem Glanz umschlungen
Da steht der Königstuhl im Odenwald
Dort füllte ich mit Frischluft meine Lungen
Und sah im Geist manch' mystische Gestalt.

Ich blickte auf das Schloß von oben -
Vergänglich war der Prinzen Herzogtum,
Die Macht der Fürsten ist zerstoben,
Die Nornen haben ihr Geschick gewoben,
Zur Sage ward der Nibelungen Ruhm.

Ruinen zeugen zwar beredt von alten Tagen,
Doch sind Symbole sie bereits vernarbter Wunden,
Wenn sie auch noch so trotzig gegen Himmel ragen
So sind sie dennoch schon naturverbunden.

Hier stritten Ritter einstens gegen Knechte
Und Völker fleischten sich in wildem Hasse
Und statt der Wahrung aller Menschen Rechte
Entwuchs noch unserem Geschlechte
Der Spottbegriff der Herrenrasse.

Mißbraucht' die Willkür auch dareinst Religionen
Sind alte Zwiste nunmehr endlich überwunden
Und zwischen vormals geifernden Nationen
Hat sich ein brüderliches Band gebunden.

Das Pfauenauge sitzt auf warmem Steine
Genießt wie wir den Ostersonnenschein
Und Vogelsang verkündet im Vereine:
Dies ist das Land von Goethe und von Heine,
Und treulich fließt der Neckar in den Rhein.

(Mannheim, April 1979)

Österreich - Austria

Wiedersehen

Altes Rathaus, Stock im Eisen
Wollen mir erneut beweisen
Daß die Stadt wo ich geboren
Mir nicht völlig ging verloren.
Als ich durch die Gassen ging -
Kärntnerstraße, Opernring -
Klingen nach die alten Lieder.
Heute sehen wir uns wieder
Und im Prater blüht der Flieder.

Hab' ich auch im Ausland Ehre,
Bürgerrechte und Karriere,
Langt's mir doch nicht aus dem Herzen
Die Erinn'rung auszumerzen
An die Freunde, an die Stätten
Die so stark an Wien mich ketten:
Philharmonikerkonzerte,
Was der Weihnachtsmarkt bescherte,
Mozartkugeln, Himbeer-Soda,
Armin Berg und Roda-Roda,
Gugelhupf, Kaffee mit Schlag,
Jugendspiele Donnerstag
Und es werden nachempfunden
Alte Freuden, alte Wunden -
So erkenne ich den Sinn
Dass ich doch noch Wiener bin.

Jetzt ist's Herbst und die Platanen
Stoßen Blätter ab und Rinde
Und die Früchte der Kastanien
Fallen ab im Abendwinde;
Doch zutiefst in meinem Herzen
Glühen noch die roten Kerzen
Der Kastanienalleen
Wie wir sie im Lenz gesehen,
Freundlich leuchtend wie im Mai,
Ist der Lenz auch längst vorbei.

(September 1988)

Mauthausener Epitaph

Gehst du am Steinbruchrand entlang
Dann denke, daß ich hier gewesen.
Ich konnt' von meiner Qual genesen
Wenn ich in diesen Abgrund sprang.

Nie hätte ich in bess'ren Tagen,
Trotz aller jugendlichen Abenteuerslust,
Geahnt, gedacht, gewollt, gehofft, gewußt,
Dass ich den Fallschirmjägersprung würd' wagen,
Selbst ohne einen Gurt zu tragen.

Die Folterknechte mögen triumphieren
Und johlen ihre haßerfüllten Lieder -
Die Spötter werden mehr als ich verlieren -
Und nächsten Frühling blüht erneut der Flieder.

(August 1988)

Die Heimat hat sich kampflos übergeben;
Noch war der Krieg nicht ausgebrochen,
Doch hat es schon nach Blut gerochen
Und meine Eltern sind nicht mehr am Leben.

Erst waren wir verstreute Emigranten,
Die hier wie drüben keine Heimat kannten
Und trotzdem war man sich im Klaren:
Es galt Prinzipien zu wahren
Und zu verneinen Hitler's Schrei
Daß Österreich nunmehr die Ostmark sei.

Es zwang uns niemand einzurücken
Und Überzeit zu machen in den Kriegsfabriken
Um der Befreiung sozusagen
Ein kleines Schärflein beizutragen.
Ich ging zurück - war es vielleicht vergebens?
Was wär' der Zweck nun meines Lebens?

Man hat mich unbegeistert wiederaufgenommen
Und staunt, daß ich dem Holocaust entkommen.
Wohl war es mir gelungen, in den Jahren
Der alten Heimat Erbe zu bewahren -
Doch will die Heimat selbst sich wiederfinden
Und forschen nach des Unheils wahren Gründen?
Drum geht es heute noch nach fünfzig Jahren;
Will wieder man in alte Bahnen fahren?

Nur wenn des Unheils Wurzeln klar gesehen
Wird unbequeme Wirklichkeit erkannt,
Nur wenn man kritisch prüft: Wie konnte es geschehen?
Wird das Gespenst von dazumal gebannt.
Wer keine Last von alten Tagen
Auf seinen jungen Schultern trägt
Der hat die Pflicht zu forschen und zu fragen
Sowie sich auch der kleinste Zweifel regt.

(August 1988)

Nicht weit von unsrem Haus in unsrer Gasse
Stand das Lokal der neuen Herrenrasse.
Ich selbst war nie in dieser Nazibude,
Zudem war auch mein bester Freund ein Jude -
Und dennoch bin ich oftmals hingegangen
Und las was dort im Fenster hatt' gehangen.

Des öftern plagt mich jetzt ein Unbehagen
Und mahnt erneut von gern vergess'nen Tagen
Als meine Heimat plötzlich anders hieß.
Oft fühle ich ein mächtiges Verlangen
Zu löschen, zu vergessen was vergangen
Als ich den Freund von meiner Türe wies.

Es ist doch leichter einfach wegzuschauen,
Zu sagen "Ich hab' niemals mitgemacht;
Ich habe nur getan was mir befohlen!"
Man schickte mich in das besetzte Polen.
Ich sah daselbst mit schweigend Grauen
Die Viehwaggons gefüllt mit Menschenfracht.

Jetzt muß ich alles nacherleben
Doch ist die Rechnung nimmer zu begleichen -
Es ist umsonst "Verjährung" anzustreben,
Umsonst, um "Ausgleich" einzureichen,
Trotz eigeninduzierter Amnesie
Und aller vorgetäuschten Phantasie
Läßt sich das tief geprägte Bild nicht streichen.

Ich bin schon jahrelang im Ruhestand
Und dennoch nie ich wirklich Ruhe fand:
Des Tags gelingt's zumal Vergang'nes zu verdrängen,
Wenn auch mit etwas weniger als Ehre,
Doch nachts marschieren die Gespensterheere
Und es beginnen sich die Wände einzuengen
Und unbewältigt bleibt was zu bewält'gen wäre.

Ich fühle oft ein unaussprechlich Langen
Zu tilgen, zu vergessen was vergangen -
Umsonst! Noch höre ich den Schritt im Kies
Als ich den Freund von meiner Türe wies.

(August 1988)

Heut heißt es Stiefel zu polieren
Zum Führereinzug aufmarschieren.
Der Sturmbannführer sagt zu mir:
"Wir machen endlich Ordnung hier.
Wenn mal der Jud die Gasse scheuert
Dann wird das ganze Land erneuert;
Zudem ist es ein grosser Spaß -
Er wird dabei ein wenig naß,
Und gibt man Säure in das Wasser
So wird er noch ein wenig blasser."

Erst wird der Jude kujoniert,
Dann seine Wohnung arisiert
Und wenn er sich dann exaltiert
Wird er nach Dachau abmarschiert.

Das war der Startschuß meines Ruhms
Und meines Kämpferheldentums.
Fragt' später mich man immerfort:
"Warst du an dem und jenem Ort?"
Ich hütet' mich, es zuzugeben
Und sprach: "In meinem ganzen Leben
Dient' ich dem Vaterland in Treue,
Daher bedarf es keiner Reue,
Denn ich war stets ein Ehrenmann
Und hab' nur meine Pflicht getan."

So konnte ich in vollen Ehren
In meine Heimat wiederkehren.
Dort wurd' ich tränenreich empfangen -
Nun gilt es, wieder anzufangen.

(August 1988)

Gefährliche Ruhe

November geht die Welt verloren
Und endlos sind die trüben Nächte
Aprilis wird sie neu geboren
Und fahles Licht erfüllt die Schächte.

Wenn schließlich warme Sonnenstrahlen
Der Erde Trost und Hoffnung geben
Und endlich auch die klagend kahlen
Platanen sich mit Grün bemalen
Regt auf der Flur ein neues Leben.

Doch kann der Lauf der Jahreszeiten
Uns selbst kein neues Sein Bereiten;
Was gestern schwer und heiß errungen
Scheint nunmehr schal und abgeklungen.

Nunmehr ergrauen unsre Haare
Und auf der Stirne stehen Falten
Doch sind wir dankbar für die Jahre
Die uns das Schicksal vorbehalten
Um sie noch sinnvoll zu gestalten.

Vielleicht denkt auch der Mensch zu viel
An alter Zeiten Gaukelspiel
Und während so die Jahre fließen
Ist's schwer die Ruhe zu genießen;
Sie ist noch weniger zu schätzen
Gäb' es kein frisches Ziel zu setzen
Und fängt man erst zu grübeln an
Dann wird die Muße selbst gefährlich,
Ein Paradox, das nicht erklärlich -
Und so ist's um die Ruh' getan.

Sieh wie die Birken sich in Winterstürmen biegen,
Sieh wie die Sonnenblumen sich im Sommerwinde wiegen -
Die Tage kriechen und die Jahre fliegen.
Der Trost am Abend unsres Lebens?
Es war vielleicht nicht ganz vergebens.

(Februar 1989)

Wo? Wann? Warum?

Wo findet man den Ring des Nibelungen?
Wohin entfloh das Lied, das einst gesungen?
Wo findet man die ungeschrieb'nen Zeilen
Der Dichter, die schon längst nicht hier mehr weilen?

Verdorren alle unerkannten Geister?
Ist alles nichterfüllte ganz verloren?
Wird das Talent zu früh verstorb'ner Meister
Erneut verliehen und erneut geboren?

In welchen parallelen Welten offenbart
Sich Mozart's Genius in ungeahnten Bahnen?
Und könnte dort ein Isaac Newton ahnen
Wie Schwerkraft sich mit andern Kräften paart?
Daß es eine Zeit gab
Wo es keine Zeit gab,
Wo jeder krasse
Begriff von Masse
Im Quantenstrom erblasse?
Wo Masse selbst, zu Energie gewandelt
Spontan sich zum Naturgesetz verwandelt
Und daß des singulären Punktes Knall -
(Noch heut erkennt man dessen Widerhall!)
Aus Nichts erschafft ein neues Weltenall?

Wenn Sternenscharen und Planeten
In rationelle Forschung treten
Dann bleibt dem armen Philosophen
Nur wenig mehr als diese Strophen.

Wie viel man auch entdecken kan
In puncto"wo?" und puncto"wann?"-
Zur letzten Frage ist man stumm:
Die letzte Frage ist: "warum?"

(November 1988)

Ausflug

Mit Singen sind wir ausgezogen -
Der Morgen war so schnell vorbei
Als hätte uns die Uhr belogen,
Als wär' der Stunden Gaukelei
Ganz im Minutentanz verflogen.

Doch steht die Sonne im Zenith
Dann ändert sich der Lauf der Zeiten:
Der Takt erstockt und wird zu Blei,
Der Stunden Fluß zu zähem Brei.

Die Sonne sinkt. Sie wirft zur Wende
Noch lange Schatten in das Tal
Und wieder geht ein Tag zu Ende.
Bald hören wir zum letzten Mal
Das längst verklung'ne Morgenlied
Als Sphärenklang
Und Abgesang -
Die Melodie der Morgenstunden
Hat nochmals Widerhall gefunden,
Sie will uns gütig Trost bereiten
Und sanft uns in den Schlaf geleiten.

Wird wohl ein neuer Tag entstehen
Wo wieder wir zum Ausflug gehen?
Man fragt und ist sich doch im Klaren:
Es wird nur einmal ausgefahren!

(Juli 1989)

Unverhoffte Frühlingswonne -
In der warmen Ostersonne
Leuchtet frische Blütenpracht.
Märzenglanz und Sommerhitze
Sind wahrhaftig schlechte Witze
Und der Wetterteufel lacht.
Denn es stürmt am nächsten Tage,
Ganz umsonst des Gärtner's Klage
Wenn der Schornstein stöhnt und kracht.

Hat sich's endlich ausgeblasen
Deckt ein Leichentuch den Rasen
Denn aus grauen Wolkenballen
Sind drei Zoll von Schnee gefallen!

Was die Jahreszeiten lehren
Kann auch uns're Weisheit mehren:
Die elysischen Gefilde
Sind für Menschen Truggebilde:
Wird man erst vom Glück geblendet
Ist der Segen schon beendet
Und des Zufalls Liebesgabe
Trägt man trauernd dann zu Grabe,
Setzt sich wohl auch still daneben,
Bettet seine Hoffnung ein,
Harrend auf ein neues Leben
Wenn in milden Sonnenschein
Selbst dem dunkelsten Verliese
Neues, frisches Grün entsprieße.

(April 1989)

Literature

(1) Dr. Aaron Zwergbaum, A 67-page report, a reprint without source reference kindly supplied by its author. With numerous footnotes, references and pictures.

(2) Alfred Heller - *"Dr. Seligmanns Auswanderung"* (Prof. Wolfgang Benz, Editor), Verlag C.H. Beck, München 1990.

(3) Gabriele Anderl (Vienna) - Four articles in "PROFIL" :
"Fluchtpunkt Mauritius", No. 28, 9.7.1990
"Särge im wahrsten Sinn", No. 29, 16.7.1990
"Der Untergang der Patria", No. 30, 23.7. 1990
"Deprimierende Ungewißheit", No. 31, 30.7.1990.

(4) Rainer Schauer - *"Tod in den Tropen"*, Die Zeit, No. 46, 8.11.1991

(5) Dr. O. Freudenheim - *"The Mauritius Case"*, Haaretz 31.8.1945.

(6) Dr. Aaron Zwergbaum - *"Mauritius Revisited"*, Publication of the World Zionist Press Service, P.O. Box 92, Jerusalem, Reference: 88/10/5/1616.

(7) Mme. Geneviève Pitot - *"The Jewish Refugees in Mauritius"*, a lecture delivered for the Société de l'histoire de l'Ile Maurice at Beau Bassin on 5.6.1990. (The notes were kindly supplied by Mme. Pitot.)

A LIST OF SOME OF THE NAMES MENTIONED IN THIS DOCUMENT

(The addresses given are mostly long out of date (R.S.L.))

Bak, Dr. Dora, 8, Queens Gate Terrace, London SW7

Bauer, Dr. Rikard, Zagreb, Preradovićeva 5

Benz, Prof Wolfgang, Fachbereich 1, Institut für Antisemitismusforschung, Technische Hochschule Berlin, Telefunkenhaus, 36 Ernst-Reuter-Platz, D1000, Berlin 10

Berger, Dr. Dora, Pension Friedwald, Achuza Shmuel, Haifa

Blum, Dr. Nelly, Vienna 8, Albertgasse 26

Bondy, Ing. Emil, Bratislava, Gärtnergasse 1, Tel. 5588

Bondy, (n.n.) c/o Arthur Thieben, Budapest 12, Zsambehi u. 10

Brüll, Alexander, Elektrostudio, Yonah Hanavi 28, Tel Aviv (the brother-in-law of Dr. Löwy's wife in Bratislava)

Cohen, Simcha, Tel Aviv, (son of the Kraffts of Bratislava)

Deutsch, Walter, c/o Niemand, Olive valley 9, Haifa

Edel, Dr. Jakob, c/o Verband der Jüdischen Kultusgemeinde, Beograd, P.O.box 599

Eisner, Paul, diamond dealer, 580, 5th Avenue, New York

Enoch, Lt Dr. Erwin, (one-time) Czechoslovak Forces, P.O.Box 281, London, EC1

Fleischmann, 18, Rue des écoles, Limoges, France

Gaspardi, (n.n.) Rue Dein 70, Antwerpen

Goldenberg, Bernhard, 95, Hodford Rd., London NW11

Harburger, Rose and Fritz, R. Shemen 8A, Hadar Hacarmel, Haifa (the son-in-law and daughter of Dr. Alfred Heller)

Heller, Dr. Alfred - see Harburger

Hirsch, Bella, c/o Segal, Herzlia, Israel

Hirschhorn, Eliahu, International Transportation, Haifa

Holzer, Lux, 2, Holland Park Avenue, London W11

Kassner, Karl, Builder, P.O. Box 487, Haifa (brother-in-law of Walter Deutsch, Vienna)

Katz, Dr. Paul, Bucurestilor 112, Cernauti, Romania (student of Dr. Robert Lenk)

Klein-Lelewer, 310, South State, Chicago, Ill., U.S.A.

Kolb, Theodore, 67, Hendon Way, London,.NW2

Koppel, Ernst, R. Brenner, 15, Tel Aviv (?) (brother of Mrs Buxbaum)

Krafft, Maximilian, Bratislava, Dr. Paul Blahogasse 31A

Kraus, Kamilla, Bratislava, Dürre Maut 3

Kraus, Ing. I., Zagreb, Vodnikova 11

Lenk, Dr. Richard, 308 W. 89th Street, Manhattan, New York

Löwith, Walter, 241, Northfield Rd., Kings Norton, Birmingham 30

Mandel, David, Bucuresti, 48 Lameneanu (a friend of the Ruppins)

Mayer, Perez B., Nof Yam, R. Hakidma 18, Herzlia, Israel

Milch, Kitty, c/o Mrs. Rudik, 263, Eastern Parkway, Brooklyn, New York (She and her parents had lived in the flat above the Lenks at Vienna 7, Schottenfeldgasse 53 before the "Anschluss")

Musskat, Dr. Alexander, Rehovoth, Israel, (a friend of Ing. Bondy)

Pichler, (n.n.), Prague 1, Vezonská 6

Pitot, Mme. Geneviève, 6380 Bad Homberg v.d.H., Hessenring 79, Germany

Pollak, Dr. Oskar, Maribor, Slovenska 39, Slovenia

Popovic, (n.n.), Preradovičeva 19, [?] (a colleague of Prof. Dr. Robert Lenk)

Rattner, Julius, 5, Claydon St., Ipswich, Suffolk (Mrs. Rattner and her husband and daughter had worked to obtain the immigration permit)

Robitschek, Fritz, c/o Fernando Wolf, Rua Dr. Pinto Ferraz, 604A, São Paulo, Brazil

Schick, Lily, Hatsafon Meshek Poalot, R. Keren Kayemet 75, Tel Aviv (daughter of Kamilla Kraus)

Silber, Aharon, c/o Yosef Silber, R. Frug 40, Tel Aviv

Silberstein, Ernst and Martha, c/o Hermann Ehrenhaft, P.O. Box 685, Haifa, or: c/o Shimshon Mayer, R. Bialik, Ramat Gan, Israel

Singer, Mrs.,(n.n.), c/o Joe Resch, 3343 Decatur Ave., Bronx, New York, or: 2796, Marion Ave., Bronx, New York

Sputz, Desider, Bánská Bistrica, Kuzmanyho ul. 2, Czechoslovakia

Tarnai, Misa, Chevrat Hapoalot, Petach Tikvah, Israel

Thalheim,Dr. Michael, c/o Dr. Pokorny, Nes Ziona 4, Tel Aviv

Till, Kurt, 15, Clarendon Rd., London W11, (nephew of Mr. Teitelbaum)

Wehle, Friedl, c/o Mrs. Barker, 18, Bruton Place, Berkeley Sq., London W1

Zwergbaum, Dr. Aaron, 58, Tchernichovsky St., Jerusalem 92585